New Realism, New Barb

Recasting Marxism

Boris Kagarlitsky

The Twilight of Globalization

The Return of Radicalism

New Realism, New Barbarism

Socialist Theory in the Era of Globalization

Boris Kagarlitsky

Translated by Renfrey Clarke

LONDON • STERLING, VIRGINIA

First published 1999 by Pluto Press
345 Archway Road, London N6 5AA
and 22883 Quicksilver Drive,
Sterling, VA 21066–2012, USA

ISBN 0 7453 1556 9 hbk

British Library Cataloguing in Publication Data
A catalogue record for this book is available from
the British Library

Library of Congress Cataloging in Publication Data
Kagarlitsky, Boris, 1958–
New realism, new barbarism : socialist theory in the era of globalization / Boris Kagarlitsky ; translated by Renfrey Clarke.
p. cm. — (Recasting Marxism)
Includes bibliographical references and index.
ISBN 0–7453–1556–9 (hbk.)
1. Post-communism. 2. Capitalism. 3. Communism. 4. Socialism.
I. Title. II. Series.
HX44.5.K34 1999
330.12'2—dc21 99–35172
CIP

Designed and produced for Pluto Press by
Chase Production Services, Chadlington, OX7 3LN
Typeset from disk by Stanford DTP Services, Northampton
Printed in the EC by TJ International, Padstow

Contents

Preface

Capitalism is in crisis, but so is the left. While the structural crisis of the capitalist world-system became visible from a commonsense perspective only in 1998 when the Asian 'tiger economies' and Russia collapsed, the crisis of the left was a permanent political factor throughout the 1990s. It started around 1989 when Soviet *perestroika*, which was seen as a great project to renew socialism, turned out to be a disastrous prelude to the restoration of capitalism. What was achieved was not the promised democratic transformation but a decline in social standards and the triumph of the mafia, which established its own regime with the full support of liberal Western powers. Socialist slogans were discredited but democratic ideals were discredited as well. Private property triumphed but respect for the law collapsed.

The international communist movement disintegrated in 1991 together with the Soviet Union. Social democracy, instead of moving into the political space vacated by its long-time communist opponents, moved further to the right.

The crisis of the left was moral and ideological rather than social. Although the left-wing vote declined somewhat internationally between 1989 and 1992, this decline was far less than the demoralization of socialist politicians and intellectuals would indicate. From 1993 the left has been becoming stronger everywhere in electoral terms. But that does not change the situation.

In the West, in Latin America and to a certain extent in Eastern Europe a whole generation of activists, intellectuals and leaders was inspired by the ideas and experiences of the great radical movements of 1968. That era ended in 1989. The spirit of 1968 evaporated. The libertarian values of the 1960s influenced the lifestyles of the emerging cosmopolitan middle class, and they were diffused through material culture by the new information technologies spreading all over the world.[1] Some of these libertarian ideas and approaches were even incorporated into the ideology of the neo-liberal right. But the movement was finally defeated.

Ideologically, 1968 was an attempt to combine libertarian culture with Marxist theory; but culture and style were absorbed by capitalism, Marxism was declared dead and the radical middle-class intellectuals, who led the movement for a couple of decades, surrendered. They either retreated into academic ghettos or accepted the 'great truth' of capitalism, or they restricted their radicalism to culture, dropping out of real political struggles. Or they disconnected their cultural struggles from the class struggle, which made cultural politics at best irrelevant, at worst reactionary.

Reform-communist intellectuals in the East, who were often ready to face persecution under the Soviet regime, were seduced by the opportunity to get rich and to be rewarded by the new authorities for their previous efforts. The new authorities were often worse than the old Soviet ones – at least Leonid Brezhnev and late-Soviet bureaucracy did not bomb their own cities, did not let their population starve. But that did not matter, or it was seen as part of the price to be paid for the 'transition to democracy'.

Surprisingly enough, those who were bombed or forced to starve did not want to pay the price. Resistance continued – in Russia as well as in Albania, in Indonesia as well as in Mexico. It was desperate, badly organized, but it was real. Only this time political intellectuals and the organised left were not part of it. Instead of leading and educating the masses, they abstained from the struggles, commenting on them, or trying to use them for narrow electoral purposes.

While *The Communist Manifesto* now reads as if it was written just a few weeks ago, the political left prefers other sources of inspiration, which are eagerly purveyed to them by the bourgeois media. At best, Marxist studies became purely academic, and the intellectuals rush around, always looking for another trendy idea which never lasts more than a year or two.

However Marxism *is* relevant and the crisis of capitalism proves that. Ironically, it is the very success of neo-liberal capitalism that is making the traditional socialist project as defined by Marx and Engels both necessary and feasible. It is not Marxism but its revisions that are becoming outdated in the era of free market capitalism and globalization. There are simple truths which must be remembered. Capitalism is a system which generates poverty and crises. It is also a system which generates class struggle and revolutionary socialist movements. If the old movement is dead, it is time for the new one to be born.

'Recasting Marxism', comprising three volumes, is an attempt to provide a general overview of the perspectives of the left and the socialist project following the shocks of the period 1989–91. Enough time has now passed for it to be possible to speak not just about the shock, but about the processes that are going on within the left itself, and which often have no particular links with the 'collapse of communism'.

In the books, I try to show how the defeat of the left has exacerbated the contradictions of capitalism, which objectively needs 'external supports' and which, throughout its history, has turned for this purpose to other social systems, both pre-capitalist and post-capitalist or socialist. The inability of leftists to issue a systematic challenge to capitalism is, in turn, a sign of their inability to reform capitalism. The anti-capitalist thrust of left ideology has been a key factor not just for the revolutionary movement, but also for effective reformism, which has sought to administer some remedies to capitalism. In forswearing anti-capitalism, leftists not only lose the ability to claim the role of forces capable of creating a new society, but also become incapable of improving the society of the present day.

The weakness of the left and the lack of forces capable of realizing a socialist project does not automatically mean that neo-liberal capitalism is strong. So long as neo-liberalism retains its ideological hegemony in society, despite proving a failure in economic terms, the only alternative to it is a new barbarism, which is becoming a reality in Eastern Europe (signs of it are also appearing in the West). To the extent that the neo-liberal hegemony has changed the overall relationship of forces in politics, this hegemony is a key topic of the book. In my view, leftists exaggerate the importance of the 'objective' aspects of the 'new reality' – that is, globalization, the weakening of the state and so forth – while underestimating the importance of the hegemony of the neo-liberal project.

This first volume *New Realism, New Barbarism*, is devoted to a discussion of the myth of 'the end of the Marxist project'. The psychological state of the left movement is characterized as one of collective neurosis giving rise to inadequate responses. The book is in essence an attempt (almost Freudian in its inspiration) to do battle against political neurosis with the help of political analysis.

The second volume (*The Twilight of Gobalization*) is concerned with the objective external limitations confronted by attempts at social transformation on the threshold of the new century. While any revolutionary or reformist project necessarily faces these limitations, the neo-liberal reactionary project faces them as well. I try to show the falsity both of the interpretation of globalization as a completely new and all-changing phenomenon, and of the attempt to treat it simply as a policy of the ruling layers and to show that there is nothing technologically or economically legitimate in it. The question is one of transforming and strengthening the state as an answer to the challenge of globalization. But the 'return of the state' to the economy will become a reality only if the state itself changes radically, along with its methods of intervening and functioning, including on the international level.

The third volume *The Return of Radicalism* is devoted to the crisis of the institutions and organizations with which the left project has traditionally been associated. It deals with the crisis of the trade unions and attempts to revive them. It deals with the emergence of the postmodernist left in the West during the 1990s. Contrary to some Western interpretations, the experience of Eastern Europe and of the Third World shows the vital need for a universalist left as the *only real alternative* to diverse forms of barbarism. And it examines the state of the contemporary left, the experience of left parties and movements of the 'new wave' such as the German Party of Democratic Socialism, the Workers' Party in Brazil and the Mexican Zapatistas. Not only the successes of these formations, but also their problems and failures, provide extremely important material for developing the strategy of the left in new conditions.

Our duty as socialists is to resist capitalism and to fight even those struggles which seem most desperate. That is the essence of duty: you do not just fight because you can win but because you have to defend your principles and values. However, as experience shows, many calculations of *Realpolitik* failed and many desperate struggles ended up in victories. For many years the left has been in retreat. I think it is about time to change this.

'Recasting Marxism' was started in 1995 when the prospects for the left seemed to be much worse than they seem now, in 1999. But not everybody shared this pessimism. During all this time I was helped and encouraged by so many people that I do not have enough space here to thank all of them. But still I must mention at least some names. I have to thank my friend and translator Renfrey Clarke, who stayed in Moscow through all these terrible frustrating years of Yeltsin regime and who did an incredible amount of work on this manuscript without even being sure that it was going to be published. I have to thank Eric Canepa, from the New York Marxist School, and Dale McKinley, an activist and theorist of the South African communist movement; I discussed the ideas of this book with both of them, and both helped me to get the right sources and necessary contacts. Naturally I have to thank my family which supported me in my effort.

And finally, I think that we all have to be grateful to the Zapatistas in Mexico and to the miners of Russian Kuzbass – for their resistance to neo-liberalism, for reviving hope.

Introduction

The New Barbarism

The last decade of the twentieth century began as a time of hope. Millions of people were captivated by the dream of a wonderful new epoch. The victory of the West over the East was perceived as the triumph of freedom and initiative. No one in the East particularly lamented their defeat in the Cold War. It seemed that prosperity was just around the corner. All that was needed was for the countries of the East to rejoin 'world civilization' and to enter the 'common European home'.

But, after only a few years, the bright hopes were replaced by scepticism. In the West today many economists and sociologists are recalling the last century of the Roman Empire. That period began with the growing feeling of weakness which was suppressed by unexpected triumphs. For a short time the Empire regained its lost confidence, but this did not last for long. That century ended in catastrophe.

The Decade of Frustration

In 1989 it seemed obvious to millions of people that the free market and private enterprise, combined with Western-style democracy, would automatically bring prosperity to all. By the mid-1990s it had not only become necessary to forget about prosperity, but Western-style democracy was also looking shaky, and was showing few signs of being able to solve its own problems. The liberal economic order, that had been proclaimed as the natural basis for political freedom, was increasingly contradicting this freedom; the voices arguing that democratic institutions should be rejected as impediments to the freedom of the market were growing louder.

The crisis that erupted in France in December 1995 showed how wide the gulf had become between the new elites and the majority of the population. The government explained that there were no alternatives to welfare cuts but the unions said 'No' and suddenly the great majority of working people joined the struggle. The media, backed by the intellectual elite, failed to convince people that they had to give up. Finally it was the government that had to retreat. And we suddenly learned that the alternative was possible. The popular uprising in the Mexican state of Chiapas in 1994 bore witness to the same phenomenon. Accepted concepts of order, law, concord and of trust in authority were placed in doubt. Journalists and sociologists who observed the Paris demonstrations remarked that people no longer perceived the state, even if democratic, as their own.

'Before the economic crises of the 1970s and 1980s, the state incorporated many aspects of the post-war "social peace" and "consensus model"', Raghu Krishnan observed in the journal *Links*:

> These aspects were adopted as a result of specific social and political struggles and because of the willingness of ruling layers to compromise in a context of strong economic growth and Cold War pressures. This was actually an exceptional period, and we are now returning to 'business as usual' as far as the history of capitalism is concerned. The state is reverting back to its 'lean and mean' role, a tool to be wielded exclusively in the interests of big business, the banks and the wealthiest layers of the population.[1]

The End of Alternatives?

Despite the unprecedented political and ideological strength of capital on a world scale, most societies display a growing instability, uncertainty and sense of crisis. Neo-liberalism has not only been unable to improve the well-being of workers (this was never its goal in any case), it has also been unable to create favourable conditions for its own rule. The defeat of neo-liberalism is no longer a question for debate. The triumph of neo-liberalism never occurred, the economic model of the free market is disintegrating before our eyes, and in the countries of Eastern Europe the words and expressions making up the liberal lexicon have taken on the force of obscenities. It would seem that the time for alternatives has now come. But where are these alternatives? And why have they not as yet been formulated?

'The individualist, laissez-faire values which imbue the economic and political elite have been found wanting – but with the decline of socialism, there seems to be no coherent alternative in the wings', states the British economist Will Hutton.[2] As one of the ideologues of 'new labourism', Hutton knows perfectly well what he is talking about. Even parties that vociferously condemn neo-liberalism remain its hostages.

When the American philosopher Francis Fukuyama declared that with the triumph of neo-liberalism the end of history had arrived, people first argued with him, then began laughing at him and finally dismissed him. This, however, was a mistake. When Fukuyama declared the end of history, he did not by any means base his thesis on the economic or social successes of capitalism. He merely argued that capitalism was 'the end point of mankind's ideological evolution'.[3] In practice, he measured the success of the victorious ideology by a single criterion: the ability of the world ruling class to destroy, suffocate, corrupt or discredit any constructive alternative to itself. If there were no alternatives to capitalism, everything would stay the same whether capitalism was good or bad. In this sense, we are now even closer to the end of history than in 1989.

The economic failure of neo-liberalism has not led and will not lead automatically to the collapse of its ideological hegemony. The elites of modern-day capitalism cannot resolve the system's objective contradictions, and cannot and do not want to solve its growing problems, but they are capable of paralysing any attempts to solve these problems on the basis of alternative approaches.

Technological development is not paralysed by social structures that are clearly outdated and increasingly absurd. Advances in technology continue; the only difference is that they cease to improve life for the majority of people. Indeed, technological development becomes a negative factor. With every turn in the spiral of technological revolution, more and more new contradictions and disproportions accumulate. Relationships become confused, the structures and systems of rule grow steadily more complex, and the processes become less and less predictable. Significant groups of the population become alienated from the economic system, not only in poor countries but also in rich ones. Moreover, these social groups lack the chance to improve their positions in the course of technological modernization, since neo-liberalism has undermined the system of universally accessible education and health care where it has existed, and, where it has not, has prevented it from being set up. This means that with every new stage of technological development the number of people who are unable to join in this process will grow, and that, for outsiders, the chance at some point of enjoying the fruits of progress will steadily diminish. In each society there are now millions of people who are doomed to second-class employment, who are excluded from civil society and who, in practice, have been cast aside from the new civilization. These people cannot be called a reserve army of labour, since the new technologies are beyond their reach. The outsiders make up an anti-systemic layer within society; accumulating the potential for hatred and protest, they are by no means always capable of self-organization, and lack their own ideology and alternatives.

The established society tries to defend itself from the growing mass of outsiders, who in many countries long ago came to exceed two-thirds of the population. Even in the rich countries we see dramatic social polarization. Politicians continue to behave as if it is only the middle class that counts. But the middle class itself in many countries is getting smaller and feels threatened. The 'repressive tolerance' of the 1960s has been replaced by repressive or coercive hegemony. The official ideologies no longer convince anyone, but this scarcely troubles the authorities, since they do not allow alternative ideologies to be propagated. Or else, such ideologies are disseminated in fragmentary form, and in this way simply demonstrate their inadequacy as genuine alternatives.

The new information technologies, which in theory have the potential to undermine the dominance of the mass media that are monopolized by the elites, themselves retain an elitist character. Even the massive spread of computers has not made them available to the slum-dwellers of Rio de Janeiro or the miners of Prokopyevsk in Central Siberia. In short, the new technologies serve not only to unite people, but also to divide them.

Paraphrasing Lenin, one could say that, despite the obvious crisis, those on top do not want change, and those underneath cannot achieve it.

The lack of a revolutionary perspective has led to a profound crisis of reformism. Nowhere have the forces of the left been prepared for the new situation. Moreover, the left is itself undergoing a deep moral crisis. Instead of an indispensable reassessment of values following the events of 1989, there has been massive ideological desertion. Serious discussion on how to interpret the traditions and values of the workers' movement in contemporary circumstances has been replaced by agitated chatter about what should replace these values.

'Modest' Socialism

Summing up the activity of the European socialist parties during the twentieth century, the British historian Donald Sassoon states with at least a hint of malicious delight: 'No one any longer, anywhere, pursues a non-capitalist path.'[4] Reformism is also in crisis.

> Socialists had run out of ideas. In the 1960s they had abandoned the aim of abolishing capitalism; in the 1970s and 1980s they proclaimed that they were the ideal managers of it. By 1989 when the Berlin Wall collapsed, the conventional reformist idea that it was necessary to possess a large public sector to countervail the negative tendencies of the private sector had evaporated from the programmes of *all* socialist parties. The privatization of the public sector, previously unthinkable even among most conservatives, came to be accepted by many socialists.[5]

The only strategy for the future that Sassoon can offer in these circumstances is ... to be 'modest'.[6]

However, it is the development of modern capitalism which makes the traditional programme of the left not only a real alternative, but quite simply the only alternative. Worshippers of the new order rejoice at the fact that the world has changed by comparison with the 1960s, but find to their dismay that it is changing still further. Meanwhile, the history of liberalism itself shows that ideas that are thought hopelessly out of date can suddenly make a very strong comeback. The world system now is in such a tangle that the only way to deal with its Gordian knot of contradictions is to slice through it. Partial reforms and gradual improvements are becoming possible only as the consequences of radical shifts in the whole structure of society and the economy. Without a broad nationalization of private capital ('the expropriation of the expropriators'), without overcoming the 'free market', it is impossible to carry out even a minimal reform of the health care system or to improve social welfare.

While the ideologues of moderation remind us of the complexity of the system, which is supposed to render any attempts at state or public intervention inconceivable and full of unpredictable risks, society itself is more and more experiencing the need for a radical simplification. This is the only way in which millions of people can restore control at least over their own lives, making their existences comprehensible and meaningful.

Most left parties, however, are not afraid of anything so much as of their own traditions. Instead of discussing what nationalization means today, they are wasting their time trying to prove to the ruling elites that there will not be any nationalizations. The ruling classes, meanwhile, have less than complete trust in these promises, and prefer not to allow leftists to gain access to the levers of real power unless these leftists have given proof of their complete political impotence.

The lack of alternatives is leading to the erosion of all forms of representative democracy. But in this case the crisis of democracy, unlike the case in Europe in the 1920s or in Latin America during the 1970s, is not leading to the rapid collapse of democratic institutions. Instead, these institutions are slowly degenerating and dying out. They are increasingly being bypassed not only by economic decision-making, but even by the political process itself.

The rebirth of fascism in Europe is an important symptom of the crisis. But what is involved is not just the rise of extreme right-wing organizations. The organizations of the political establishment itself are increasingly becoming infected with authoritarian populism. This is only natural in circumstances where trust in the institutions of representative democracy has been undermined.

The Arrogant 'Civilization'

A crisis without an alternative is a sign of imminent shocks. In this sense the catastrophe in Rwanda provides humanity with a warning. The West should not comfort itself with the hope that the hunger, bloodshed and economic collapse on the periphery will not touch the centre.

The fall of the civilizations of antiquity also began with collapse on the periphery. In this respect, the past has a terrible lesson to teach us. The 'end of history' is not a foolish joke by a person who has read too much Hegel, but a real possibility. Of course, what is at stake is only our own history and our own present-day society. Humanity as a biological species has survived the fall of a series of civilizations. It will also survive the collapse of the 'global' bourgeois civilization of our time.

If Western Europeans and North Americans are the new Romans, then others of us – Eastern Europeans, Latin Americans, Africans and Asians – who live on the periphery of the Western world must be the new barbarians. This might seem like a bad joke, but people shouldn't laugh.

World civilization knows two types of relations between societies. Either one civilization withstands the impact of another, or else everything is reduced to the counterpositing of 'civilization versus the barbarians'. The question is not about whose society, ranked on the basis of 'richer is better', is more developed. So long as one society lives in isolation from another, these comparisons are pointless. But even when interaction is inevitable, it can occur in various ways.

Coming into contact with Europe, the Chinese and Japanese could not deny the superiority of European technology. Nor could they avoid seeing the effectiveness of European political institutions. All this had to be interpreted, evaluated and as far as possible made use of. But the East nevertheless saw itself as a different civilization compared to the West. Not worse, not better, but simply different. In exactly the same way, Soviet society as well perceived itself as a different civilization from the West, even during the 1980s the talk was of 'dialogue', 'interpenetration' and 'convergence'. This signified that there were two cultures and two types of society, each living according to its own rules. These rules underwent changes, but the changes had to come from within, expressing the particular needs and traditions of the societies concerned.

With the collapse of the Soviet system, the belief of former Soviet citizens in their own special civilization collapsed as well. A new formula emerged. Civilization was represented by the West. There was the 'civilized world', consisting of 'civilized countries'. We had to 'join' or 'enter' this world, to 'retrace our steps'. Since they had won and we had lost, we had no choice but to become like them.

Even the most primitive tribe has its own values and culture. There are established institutions that are supposed to be respected. But once the encounter with 'civilization' shows the ineffectiveness of these institutions, everything changes. The vanquished see themselves as barbarians.

And so, if they represent civilization, we must be barbarians. This revolution in perceptions of the world begins with the loss of self-respect, with the devaluation of everything which is familiar and which is felt to be one's own. They live; we merely exist. They enjoy progress; we have stagnation. They are fully realized human beings, while we are creatures of an inferior order, 'deformed' by our 'incorrect' social experience, false ideology and totalitarian state system.

This is not only the case in Eastern Europe. Even in South Korea, when in 1997–8 the Asian financial crisis erupted, economists started writing about the importance of becoming Western: 'at the root of Korea's national crisis is a deeply embedded cultural irrationality', 'Korean society still includes aspects of the irrational, and if this persists, Korea will never be able to adopt the western European model of capitalism.'[7] To become 'rational' one should adopt unemployment, free competition and the unrestricted rule of private property.

In this case it is not important whether the propositions advanced are true. As it happens, each of the formulas contains a portion of truth, along with a generous helping of conscious and unconscious falsehood. One way or another, these assertions complement one another and combine together to form a definite system of ideas, expressing the self-perception and sense of self-worth of the barbarian.

Two civilizations can conduct a dialogue. Barbarians, however, cannot call into question – or even seriously discuss – the principles of a civilization. All they can do is to reproduce its forms.

Naturally, barbarians assimilate an alien civilization in barbarian fashion. To the degree that barbarians join a civilization, the civilization itself becomes barbarized. The external attributes of the alien civilization are the first elements to be borrowed. They are seen as magic symbols of success. Barbarians put on togas or European uniforms, or install computers in their offices.

Encountering an alien civilization, barbarians see the results of its functioning, and try to reproduce them with minute precision. They copy the petty details, the secondary characteristics. The secret of success, however, escapes them. This is because the secret does not lie in mechanically duplicating the actions of others. A civilization has lived its own life, and has undergone its own development. The 'secret' behind a civilization lies in the history of its development. The result cannot be reproduced unless one reproduces, down to the smallest details, all the twists, turns and stages of the society's previous development. This, of course, is inconceivable. Repeating an alien process of development is just as impossible as living someone else's life.

If the secret of success lies in development, the reasons for the effectiveness of one or another set of structures have to be sought in the history of these structures, in the circumstances of their origin. Receiving a ready-made result, the barbarian hopes to immediately 'join' the heights of civilization, but often receives no more than the products of its decay. Trying to copy the result means dooming yourself to catastrophe. It is always the same story, repeating itself again and again throughout history. The foundations for the greatness of Rome were laid during an epoch when no one took the small Italic republic seriously. But barbarian princelings paraded in the togas of emperors, without understanding why no one was willing to pay them any attention. They imitated the final form which impressed them most. The substance, the history were not even examined. Later, the faithful admirers of the USSR in Africa founded one-party systems, set up provincial and regional party committees on the Soviet model, and were then astonished when Soviet-level industry, medicine, education and science failed to materialize along with them. These admirers of the USSR copied the Soviet practices of the 1970s, and did not guess that by this time the Soviet system was merely reaping the fruits of the tragic efforts of previous decades.

Today our new barbarians are conscientiously setting up joint-stock companies, stock exchanges and banking groups, while forgetting that the victorious capitalism of the time of Adam Smith knew nothing of any of this. Its success represented the triumph of petty shopkeepers and small-time individual entrepreneurs who never used even the term 'securities'.

The products of crisis are perceived as symbols of success. We receive all the ailments of the ageing social organism without grasping the secret of its earlier growth. For the barbarian, civilization is above all 'Western levels of comfort'. But comfort is rarely combined with dynamism. Brocade and gold, the creations of Roman jewellers, Mercedes cars and holidays in five-star hotels are the first things needed by the 'new proprietors'. The founders of capitalism sacrificed everything in order to pursue their goals, just like American pioneers, Soviet commissars or the legionaries of Scipio. The protestant ethic forbade light-minded diversions, games of chance and irresponsible risk-taking. These were all traits of the decadent aristocracy. The legionaries despised the luxurious courts of the Hellenic East, and the Bolsheviks quite rightly saw in such pampered living a sign of the decay of the bourgeois West; if the members of the bourgeoisie came to resemble the aristocrats, that meant that in the near future they would share their fate.

In general, there is no truer symbol of imminent collapse than the cult of gambling. It was no accident that the spread of capitalism in Russia began not with the triumph of the protestant ethic, but with the appearance of thousands of casinos and of innumerable companies that turned business into a game of roulette. The *nomenklatura*, which had lost the traditions of social responsibility, was enraptured at being able to explore the seductions of 'Western civilization'.

Barbarians cannot develop independently; they can only imitate, plunder and destroy. The more we try to 'enter into world civilization', the more we become barbarians. And the more we become barbarians, the more dangerous we are to our neighbours, to ourselves and to the West. The world lived in relative peace and prosperity for decades while under threat of nuclear annihilation. Yugoslavia did not pose a danger to anyone in Europe, while in the Arab world no one knew of populist politicians like Vladimir Zhirinovsky who promise their admirers to launch 'a last push to the south' and lead Russian troops to the Indian Ocean. Italians had not even heard of the 'Russian mafia'. The challenge of the new barbarism, the unrealizable dream of 'joining Western civilization', means chronic instability and a whole parade of catastrophes, disappointments and conflicts. The whirlpool of instability draws in more and more new regions and countries. No one's safety is guaranteed, and no one's interests are reliably protected.

The Barbarians at the Gates

Full of self-satisfaction at having proven its superiority to the barbarians, civilization refuses to clasp them to its bosom. The more that barbarians admire civilization, the greater their disappointment and indignation at being shut out of it. Eastern Europeans in the 1990s suffered a shock when they discovered that the countries of the West, while demanding that their new allies imitate and admire them, were in no hurry to integrate these allies into the Western economic and political structures. The Maastricht and Schengen agreements, which for the West became symbols of a drawing together of peoples, were perceived in the East as new symbols of the division of the continent. The bitterness of these disappointments was expressed by Bulgarian intellectuals appealing to their Western colleagues:

> We all have spent a long time living in a separated world. We dreamed about a free society where we could satisfy our artistic curiosity by visiting each other, accumulating creative stimuli, expanding our experience and opportunities of the audiences to face a broader range of work. It was our dream of a world without borders, which kept us positive in the shade of the Iron Wall. If only the Great Liberation Day would come!
>
> The Day came, and passed. And nothing happened.
>
> Once it was the Wall. Today it is the economic crisis. Once it was the fear of communist censorship. Today it is the phlegm of a totally disintegrated and desperate society. To make things even worse there came the notorious Schengen treaty.
>
> We are in the check-in lounge again. We sit on our suitcases and look forward to crossing borders.[8]

Imitating civilization is only the first stage. Knowing that their hopes have been deceived, but not understanding why, the barbarians become aggressive. Their striving to 'join civilization' remains, but their approach changes. Now, if it is impossible simply to introduce civilization to their countries, the possibility that remains for them is to appropriate its fruits.

There are striking similarities between the last triumphs of Rome in the fourth century and the last triumphs of the West in the years from 1989 to 1991. In each case these triumphs were somewhat unexpected; they were preceded not by a series of successes, but by a period of uncertainty and crisis, which was suddenly replaced by a new, aggressive self-confidence. It might now seem that the West has regained its former dynamism. But this is an illusion. After world hegemony has been attained and there are no adversaries who might contest it, all that remains is to decide how to rule the dramatically expanded periphery. Triumph, however, is followed by confusion. The legions might still inspire fear, but they cannot control the situation. On the outskirts of the empire, chaos increases, feeding discord back to the centre.

The American economist Lester C. Thurow, comparing the contemporary West with the late Roman Empire, observes that the fall of Rome began not with military defeats, but with a situation in which 'the public was squeezed out by the private'.[9] Today's world is experiencing the same phenomenon. The bases for the rise of Rome had been public morality and public enterprise, but after the empire had crushed its main enemies everything changed. The result was not the flowering of individuality and the triumph of free initiative, but the collapse of society and the beginning of the dark ages, developments which made any form of entrepreneurship pointless.

The West cannot change, and has no wish to change, the system under which the prosperity of the wealthy countries of the centre rests on the humiliation and exploitation of the countries of the periphery. This is also one of the secrets of the 'success' of civilization. The culture, and the very existence, of the inhabitants of the barbarian world are valued less than the life of a 'civilized human being'. And for the barbarian, civilization promises no other fate apart from dependency and subjugation. But even after becoming reconciled to the fate of his or her people, every person wants the best for himself or herself. Millions of people make their way toward the population centres of the empire. The first barbarians arrive as emigrants and even as honoured guests. They are invited; they are needed for their labour power, as hired workers. And finally, they come as representatives of 'local elites'. The emperors arrange for Germans and Goths, wishing to 'join' the empire, to cross the Rhine. The Berlin Wall is ceremoniously demolished. American ships pick up Cuban refugees. Mexico is included in the North American free trade zone.

Very soon, however, the streams of immigrants become so large that no empire could ever cope with them. The 'centres' try to shut themselves off from the periphery. Barriers are erected. Once again, the frontier is under lock and key. The struggle against illegal immigration comes to figure among the crucial tasks of the state. But the flood of immigrants can no longer be stopped. Millions of despairing people, pressed onward by other, still more despairing people, break down all obstacles. They organize themselves, learn to resist, become conscious of their interests and rights.

Behind the peaceful immigrants come the warriors. The more 'civilization' is closed off from the barbarian invasion, the more frequent and bloody the clashes become. By now the forces of the centre are no longer able to withstand the onslaught of the periphery. Civilization collapses. The barbarians remain on their own. They have lost their former respect for their own traditions and values; now they also cease to believe in the civilization whose 'weakness' has been exposed.

When in 1999 the war broke out between Yugoslavia and the West, civilized Europeans and Americans blamed barbarian Serbs and their authoritarian government for everything that happened. True, the Serb government was cruel. But the West itself acted in a brutal, irresponsible and cynical way. The West promised 'humanitarian intervention' to stop barbarian conflicts in the Balkans. It brought even more suffering, death, destruction.

Happy to have high technologies, American military and politicians bombed office buildings in Belgrade promising minimal civilian casualties. 'And of course, we all felt good that our bombs didn't blow up that maternity hospital next door, but merely forced mothers and their newborn babies to flee in panic', commented a left-wing journalist Joel McNally. 'Another example of good old American know-how at avoiding direct hits on maternity wards.'[10]

Unfortunately even that was not true. As the war continued, we learned more about passenger trains being hit, refugees being killed by the very force which promised 'humanitarian intervention'.

Western civilization tried to prove its superiority to barbarians by using the most sophisticated technology of destruction. But even that did not work. Low-tech barbarians fought back with their primitive weapons, medieval, irrational determination and courage. And the civilized forces of the West discovered that their expensive war toys cannot always match that. Civilization, after all, was attractive to the barbarians because of its victories; it was because of these victories that the vanquished came to account themselves beings of a lower order, and stopped believing in their own gods. Now all this belongs to the past. Civilization created the barbarians; the barbarians have destroyed civilization. The dark ages begin.

Politicians and journalists take cover behind generalities about 'ethnic conflicts', as though the economic and social order had nothing to do with these struggles. No one, however, can explain why it should be in the late twentieth century, with the onset of the era of 'freedom', 'democracy' and the 'market economy', that peoples and communities who earlier coexisted more or less peacefully are flinging themselves into attempts at mutual extermination. Hutus and Tutsis, Serbs and Croats have never shown much love for one another, but it is far from true that this has always led to bloody clashes between them.

Building the Pyramids

The new economy destroys social bonds, the traditional norms and patterns of authority, and inspires aggressiveness. In the view of Mrs Thatcher, the main heroine of the neo-liberal myth, society does not exist. Theory is transformed into practice. Where society is disintegrating, there remain only the bonds of kinship, the 'voice of blood'. There are no mutual obligations, and there cannot be trust in 'aliens'. The category of aliens, meanwhile, comes to encompass all the rest of humanity.

Explaining social chaos on the basis of 'ethnic' causes was only possible until the Albanian unprising of 1997. Here the failure of the policies of neo-liberal capitalism appeared in all its stark concreteness. As late as December 1994 International Monetary Fund head Michel Camdessus included Albania in a list of countries where 'significant progress' was supposed to have been made toward macro-economic stabilization, and where 'substantial reforms' were said to have been implemented. 'Prodigious efforts and remarkable results', Camdessus argued, had been seen in Albania, 'this small country, the poorest in Europe ...'[11] Numerous Western delegations and consultants visited the Albanian capital, Tirana, and expressed great satisfaction with what they observed. A 'Miss World' contest was even being held in the city. What was really happening, however, was plainly visible even from the international airport.

> The narrow, pot-holed road from the airport to the capital presents the arriving visitor with a spectacle that is perhaps one of the most miserable to be seen in flourishing Europe. Signs of general desolation and ruin are to be met with at every step.

According to this Russian journalist not only most of the people on the rutted streets, but even the animals in the zoo, sitting behind thick bars 'on the bare floors of tiny cages', appeared half-starved.[12]

Most of industry was at a standstill, and the most prosperous sector was the construction of financial pyramids. These were strengthening their position by conducting illegal trade in weapons and petrol with neighbouring Yugoslavia, blockaded by the world community, and also by laundering money for the Italian mafia. All this was continuing beneath the gaze of the Western experts. It was only in October 1996, four months before the crash, that the latter were moved to express certain misgivings.

So great was the sympathy in the West for the Albanian regime of Sali Berisha that the embassies of Western countries studiously closed their eyes to human rights violations, election-rigging, corruption and even the breaching of international sanctions against Yugoslavia. Socialist leader Fatos Nano was thrown into prison, and opposition parties were prevented from operating freely. Meanwhile, a journalist from the Albanian opposition wrote:

> the West looked the other way and applauded Albania's market reforms, thus indicating to the general public that they

> supported Berisha and his policies. The international community was willing to give him the benefit of the doubt, and excused human rights violations as mere 'isolated cases' in transitional times.

The hypocrisy was conscious, consistent and cynical, and became obvious to everyone when the West approved the rigging of local elections in October 1996. 'The Western European embassies released their official statements on the elections before the monitors returned from the field.'[13] Only later the same sources revealed that there was massive electoral fraud. And they knew about it.

It was not only in Albania that financial pyramid schemes enjoyed spectacular success. The same happened in Russia, with the well-known firm MMM, and in the Czech Republic, Poland and Romania. The ideologues of neo-liberalism had nothing to do but to write opinion articles for the *Wall Street Journal* or the *Moscow Times* trying vainly after the event to prove that the pyramids had been nothing to do with them. Why didn't they condemn these practices earlier? Not only were these retrospective self-justifications hypocritical – instead of campaigning against the pyramids, the neo-liberal ideologues had encouraged their growth, regarding them as a mechanism for 'the accumulation of capital' – but the ideology of the financial pyramids was a logical consequence of the triumph of the neo-liberal outlook on social life. And were the pyramids in Eastern Europe so different from the overvalued stock on Wall Street itself?

Most people had come to believe in the idea of personal enrichment. They were searching not for a collective, but for an individual way out of the crisis. But millions of people, even if acting individually, nevertheless constitute a social mass. Each of them acts quite independently, but all of them do one and the same thing. Production has collapsed, and in the conditions of a declining economy small business has no chance. Such absurd projects as financial pyramids were ideally suited to the new ideology that triumphed in Eastern Europe with the fall of the communist regimes. The largest Albanian pyramid, Vefa, advertised itself as 'genuine capitalism'.[14] Perhaps its owners were not altogether wrong.

The investors never made up a united whole. Each of them hoped to get out before the pyramids crumbled. Each was quite ready to build his or her fortunes on the ruin of others. But the pyramids collapsed, and everyone was ruined. The protests of the swindled Albanian investors turned into a general popular uprising. This was not a proletarian revolution, but a revolt by the declassed masses. It could not have been anything else in a country where production had collapsed, traditional bonds had been weakened and left ideology had been discredited.

When the people of Albania rose up in the spring of 1997 the Socialist leaders, who had been brought hurriedly into the government, could not find anything better to do than to appeal for help to the same 'international community' that bore prime responsibility for the disaster that had befallen the country. The left had lost its political will. Instead of joining the revolt and seeking to lead it, the members of the left showed themselves to be unwilling and unable to take the power which had virtually fallen into their hands.

The demoralization of the left does not end class struggle or abolish social contradictions. But if socialists themselves do not believe in an alternative, neo-liberalism will be confronted not with political protest but with elemental rage. Where there should be opposition, the crisis of left ideology has created a vacuum, and this vacuum is giving birth to chaos. Albania in March 1997 was like Russia in February 1917, but without Bolsheviks and without even Mensheviks. The working class was not only declassed as a result of mass unemployment and economic chaos, but had lost its tradition of struggle and its political culture, the only factors that might have helped it in these circumstances. In 1999 another crisis errupted in Romania. Again there were crouds of angry workers on the streets fighting with the police. But the left was not leading anything. It was not even present.

The only answer is the self-organization of the people. The armed masses are setting up committees, and are trying to impose order in their own ranks. But spontaneous self-organization has its own natural limits. Any uprising is accompanied by destruction. The political powerlessness of a demoralized opposition turns inevitable social upheavals into national catastrophe.

The IMF experts, together with embassy officials, quickly climbed into helicopters and fled from Tirana as rebellion engulfed the city. From time to time these helicopters came under fire from the ground. What else could have been expected, after what the 'civilized world' had done to this small, poor country? The West looked on in horror at what was occurring; it had been forced to reckon with the fruits of its own policies.

After Albania there was the Asian crisis, then the Russian rouble collapsed. Latin American currencies followed the rouble. IMF functionaries rushed around the world telling everyone their side of the story. They repeated them at the hearings of the American Congress and during their meetings with the Russian authorities. Their friends published articles in the *Wall Street Journal* and the *Washington Post.* It was an American journalist Fred Hiatt who coined the formulae which should become the IMF motto: 'to acknowledge the failure is not quite the same as saying the policy was wrong'.[15] In other words: you should not blame the good guys from the West. Every time something went wrong it was because of the stupid barbarians who did not follow the rules of capitalism properly and misinterpreted the proposals of Western advisers; or local people and bureaucrats sabotaged the necessary reforms. By the end of 1998 it was not possible to go on saying this. The best pupils of the West, the IMF's 'success stories' started falling apart. After Russia it was Brazil's turn to collapse. It was a textbook case of a 'successful financial stabilization', there was a model 'team of reformers' in power – and then suddenly everything went wrong. The Russian scenario was repeated down to minor details. Even the West was no longer immune to recession and decline. The mood in the media changed. 'If Brazil played by market rules and lost, maybe it was the wrong game to start with', complained an American journalist.[16] Instead of deregulation the IMF suddenly declared 'a shift in attitudes to controls on capital movements'.[17] Suddenly they learned that public regulation was not such a bad thing. Even the *Economist,* discussing the case of Japan, argued that a good and credible anti-crisis plan 'must involve the nationalisation of the weaker banks, perhaps 10 or even ... all the top 19'.[18] In Hong Kong, another model capitalist economy, the government had to intervene in the stock market. It made some profit and finally acquired 7.3 per cent of the 33 companies that make up the Hong Kong stock exchange.

Capitalism faced the global crisis. And the West suddenly discovered that it also had to pay the bills. George Soros, one of the richest people in the world, started to worry about the future of America. 'The global capitalist system which has been responsible for the remarkable prosperity of this country in the last decade is coming apart at the seams.'[19]

The collapse of civilization takes place where there is no alternative. Undervaluing our own lives, and characterizing the experience of the twentieth century as a meaningless impasse, we have not only let slip our chance to undertake a genuine reform of our society, and to lend it a new dynamism, we have also put in question the future of Western civilization.

Nevertheless, there is a basis for optimism in the often demonstrated ability of various societies to find a solution even where organized political forces, traditional institutions and generally recognized elites have shown their total bankruptcy. In such a situation the spontaneous resolving of contradictions 'from below' is accompanied by the collapse of all these institutions and elites. What this signifies is shocks on the scale of those of the ill-fated epoch from 1914 to 1945. Albania in the late 1990s is simply showing many other countries something of their possible – though not inevitable – future.

Forecasts of a 'sunset of Europe' have been made often enough in the past, and Europe continues to develop. But it should not be forgotten that after Spengler forecast the decline of European civilization, Europe was convulsed by war, revolutions and the rise of fascism. With hindsight, one can be glad that civilization, after surviving shocks and crises that wiped out millions of people, is proving able to rejuvenate itself, although, to be sure, this is not much consolation for the people who live in the periods of catastrophe.

Such epochs demand not moderation but radicalism; not modest but ambitious projects, not slow, gradual steps, but decisive actions. Millions of people whose interests lie in change have neither an ideology, nor a programme, nor organization. Everything that was created earlier has been devalued, has become obsolete or corrupt. It is easy to fall into hopelessness. But it is necessary to move forward.

1

The Left As it Is

The 1980s were bad years for the left. European socialist parties were already in crisis, but this crisis became incomparably more acute by the mid-1990s, following the collapse of the communist movement. The presidency of Mitterand in France began with fine hopes and ended in universal disappointment. The failure of the most serious reformist project in post-war Western history makes it imperative to rethink the question of the possibilities and prospects of reformism. No less striking was the collapse of Soviet *perestroika,* which can also be described as a sort of reformist project, and which had a very strong, although also short-lived influence on all of world left culture.

The French socialists not only lost their parliamentary majority, but had in practice rejected their own reformist project even before the right returned to power. They prepared the ground for the presidency of Jacques Chirac, who not only abolished most of the innovations of the first years of the socialist government, but also annulled many of the social gains of the previous decades. *Perestroika* in the Soviet Union culminated in the collapse of the Soviet state itself, and in the coming to power of the most decadent section of the old *nomenklatura.*

Electoral Successes, Political Failures

The political history of the left in the 1980s and the first half of the 1990s might at first glance seem like an unbroken chain of defeats. The fall of the Berlin Wall was accompanied by the disappearance of the world communist movement. In Eastern Europe, the only more or less traditional Communist Party that survived was that of the Czech Republic; this country also has a Left Bloc founded by supporters of a more radical renewal of the party, as well as a revived social democracy. In every other case, the communist organizations underwent a swift transformation. In most cases the new parties declared themselves to be social democratic, while retaining their former leaders and traditions. At the same time, social democracy in the West was undergoing a profound crisis, and moving increasingly to the right.

On closer examination, however, the picture is somewhat more complex. Throughout this period there were also electoral successes and victorious strikes. Most parties of the left and trade unions experienced difficulties, but some of them nevertheless grew. Moreover, from the mid-1990s a contrary trend became evident. Despite all the avowals of crisis, the left during the 1990s generally did well electorally once the shocks of the first years of the decade were past. After losing power, the social democrats in the Scandinavian countries quickly regained it. The right-wing forces that had long held power in Denmark suffered a crushing defeat in 1993. In Eastern Europe the post-communist parties also recovered quickly after the shock dealt to them by the fall of the Berlin Wall. With the exception of the Czech Republic, they returned to power almost everywhere free elections were held. In Italy the old communist dream of victory over the Christian Democrats came to pass. The elections of 22 April 1996 brought a convincing victory to the left-centrist Olive Tree Alliance, which won a majority not only in the parliament but also in the senate; for the first time in the country's history, a left bloc came to power. In 1997 the British Labour Party returned to power after many years in opposition, and at the French parliamentary elections a few weeks later the socialists had their revenge for the defeat they had suffered in the poll for the presidency. A year later, German Social Democrats emulated the success of their British and French counterparts.

Despite the extremely moderate views of the 1997-model British labourites, their victory (perhaps against their wishes) had a radicalizing effect on millions of people in other European countries from France to Russia. After 18 years in power, the British conservatives had become a symbol of the impregnability of capitalism and of the invincibility of the neo-liberal project. As it turned out, the conservatives were not simply beaten but routed. The subsequent French elections were striking not only for the unexpected victory of the Socialists, but also for the strengthening of the position of the Communist Party and for the record number of votes gained by the far left (and, for that matter, by the extreme right-wing National Front).

The Brazilian Workers' Party did not come to power, but dramatically strengthened its positions in parliament and in local government. In Uruguay, Colombia and Chile leftists also improved their positions. In El Salvador in March 1997 the Farabundo Martí National Liberation Front gained a decisive victory in municipal elections and sharply increased its representation in parliament. The Western news agencies reported with irritation that the leftists had 'won at the ballot box what they could not win in twelve years of civil war: control of the capital and dozens of seats in congress'.[1]

In 14 national elections in Latin America between 1993 and 1995 the left won an average of 25 per cent of the vote, an unquestioned historical record for the continent. It is significant that gains were made not only by radical but also by moderate parties. At a meeting of left organizations that attended the São Paolo Forum in 1995 it was announced that member parties had won more than 300 deputies' seats, 60 senate positions and several provincial governorships, not to speak of hundreds of mayoralties and thousands of seats on municipal councils. As noted by Marco Aurelio García, one of the leaders of the Brazilian Workers' Party (PT), for the first time in Latin America 'in almost all cases, the left and centre-left forces fought the elections with a real chance of winning'.[2] Particularly significant was the success of the Urugayan Frente Amplio, which won control of the municipality in Montevideo, the national capital, which is home to half the country's population. In Venezuela the radical party Causa R succeeded in breaking the political tradition of two-party oligarchic rule and in transforming itself into a national political force.

In South Africa the African National Congress came to power in a bloc with the Communist Party. Communists were victorious in elections in Nepal, and even received an offer to form the government in India. True to the principles of Maoism, the 'Marxist' Communist Party refused to head a bourgeois government. At the same time as testifying to dogmatism and fear of accepting responsibility, this decision was also proof of an intellectual honesty that was lacking in the case of the European post-communists, who never turned down a chance to take power. The left in India was punished, becoming the main loser in the twelfth general election to the Indian parliament in 1998. The United Front, a conglomeration of 13 national and regional parties including four mainstream left parties (the Left Front) received a massive drubbing. The election marked a gradual shrinkage in the electoral base for both communist parties, especially in the states where the left traditionally commanded considerable strength. However, in several Indian states, leftists remain the decisive force in local politics. For example, the Communist Party (Marxist) has held power in West Bengal since 1977 as the leading force in the Left Front. And while the mainstream left gets weaker the radical 'Marxist-Leninist' Communist Party (Liberation) is growing.

Electoral successes, however, do not signify in any way that the crisis of the socialist movement has been overcome. The fact is simply that the crisis has nothing to do with the supposed electoral weakness, 'narrowness' or 'disappearance' of the left's social base. On the contrary, it stems from the political impotence of leftists who, for lack of a clear strategy, contrive to turn even victory into defeat.

Donald Sassoon, in his history of socialism, notes that leftists historically have embraced two central ideas: regulation and resistance to capitalism.[3] In the late 1980s the will to practise regulation was transformed into mere vague desires, since socialists feel a sort of superstitious dread before the might of transnational corporations. They perceive globalization not as a socio-economic process with a complex dynamic, with structural contradictions and particular strong and weak points, but as an irreversible turning-point, an evil visitation, an invasion by an incomprehensible and insuperable force. This has also paralysed their will to resist. Nevertheless, resistance to capitalism continues. From being organized, however, it has become spontaneous, and from being political it has become social. The masses are more radical than the ideologues, who, out of inertia, refer to the 'conservatism' of the masses.

However improbable it might seem, the behaviour of left politicians and activists compels the suspicion that we are dealing with a collective neurosis. Right-wing social democrats feel totally impotent. Meanwhile, left socialists and communists dream of becoming right-wing social democrats. They are prevented from doing so only by their own past, which has to be overcome at any cost. Wherever left socialists, through the use of radical slogans, abruptly increase the number of their supporters, they renounce their own ideas, hoping to acquire 'respectability' and to prove their inoffensiveness to the ruling elites. The net result, however, is that they lose their supporters, after which the ruling elites also lose all interest in them. This is what happened with the left socialist parties in Scandinavia in the early 1990s. A dramatic rise in the influence of radical parties was followed by a no less dramatic slump, resulting from efforts by these parties to bring about a change of image and to demonstrate their 'responsibility'. In Denmark in the late 1980s the Socialist People's Party gained 12 per cent of the votes in parliamentary elections, but by 1994 its support had fallen to 7.3 per cent. Seeking to prove its respectability, the party renounced its fundamental opposition to European integration for the sake of participating in a national compromise. The result for the party was catastrophic. As the Danish sociologist Niels Finn Christiansen notes, the party 'disarmed itself politically. Repudiated by its voters, it has lost few members, but is no longer the independent force it was in the past.' The party's continuing existence alongside the traditional social democracy 'is now more an effect of the electoral system, and a question of style and history, than of essential political difference'.[4]

Much the same thing happened in Norway, where the Socialist Left Party in the early 1990s had the support of 12 to 15 per cent of the population. Scenting power, the socialists turned abruptly to the right, softened their opposition to NATO and the European Union, and supported Western military intervention in the former Yugoslavia. As Finn Gustavsen, one of the party's founders, admitted, the party is moving 'toward left social democratic positions', a shift which could lead to 'a total rejection of Marxist culture'.[5] The result: the party's support among voters has slipped to 7.9 per cent.

The 'Green Lefts' (*Groenlinks*) in Holland achieved a sensational success in 1989 when they won 7 per cent of the votes. In the parliamentary elections in 1994 their vote dropped by half. More right-wing Greens, running separately, could gather only 0.16 per cent.

These defeats cannot be put down to 'the effect of 1989', since during the years from 1989 to 1992 the position of the left socialists remained solid. The decline began later, and stemmed from the policies that were put forward. Nor can the turn to the right by the Danish Socialist People's Party be explained as the result of pressure from the party's social base. After the socialists began demonstrating their moderation, disillusioned voters turned to more radical groups. The result was that for the first time in many years communists appeared in the parliament, in a bloc with Trotskyists and former Maoists. In elections on 21 September 1994 the social democrats and socialists lost votes, while the 'united list' of left radicals scored important successes, winning six seats. In Holland, against the background of the defeat of the Green Lefts, the tiny ex-Maoist Socialist Party doubled its support, receiving 1.35 per cent of the votes. Another organization that strengthened its position was the left-centrist group Democracy 66, which, unlike the social democrats of the Labour Party, did not take part in the governing coalitions.

A radical bloc also won parliamentary representation in Norway. But the Party of the Centre (the former agrarians), which came out strongly against the European Union and the Maastricht Treaty, received 17 per cent of the votes in 1993 and, as acknowledged by journalists, became 'the real winners in the elections'.[6] It is not hard to work out that the votes received by the Party of the Centre were lost by the Socialists and Social Democrats.

The Swedish Left Party underwent a severe crisis in the early 1990s and almost lost all its seats in parliament, but by the middle of the decade had unexpectedly doubled its number of supporters. When Sweden for the first time elected deputies to the European parliament, the Left Party received 12.92 per cent of the votes. The fact that the Greens won a further 17.22 per cent shows how dissatisfied voters were with the 'realistic' policies of the social democrats who had regained power. The combined increase in the vote for the Greens and the Left Party amounted to 18.7 per cent, while the social democrats lost 17.2 per cent. Meanwhile the right-wing parties, which in the past had usually gained from a weakening of the social democrats, this time lost votes as well. In the 1998 parliamentary election, while Social Democrats lost votes, the Left Party repeated its success and got more than 12 per cent. Social Democrats could no longer stay in power without a formal agreement with the forces to the left of them. The surge in influence of the Left Party, however, owed nothing to active struggle. Quite the contrary; the dominant mood inside the party was of confusion and uncertainty.

The Sandinista National Liberation Front in Nicaragua remained the country's largest party after losing power in 1990. The policies of the right-wing government of Violeta Chamorro brought a rapid fall in living standards for the majority of working people. Spending on health care declined from US$35 per head of population in 1990 to US$14 in 1996, while infant mortality rose from 58 to 72 per thousand.[7] Just as they had everywhere else in the world, the neo-liberal economists promised a quick cure for the economy during the first hundred days after state regulation gave way to 'the invisible hand of the market'. A hundred days after the beginning of the reform the country was on the brink of total chaos. The government was forced to hit the brakes and even to go into reverse. In October 1990 it signed an accord with the Sandinistas and the trade unions that went under the name of 'concentration'.

The growth of discontent created real prospects for the return of the Sandinistas to power. However, the Sandinista leadership was itself drawn into privatization, while in the parliament the Sandinista deputies, proclaiming their 'responsibility', supported the government of Chamorro's prime minister Antonio Lacayo. The policy of concentration, implemented with the agreement and participation of the Sandinistas, perhaps made it possible to avoid the absolute extremes of the 'savage market', but on the whole it was permeated by the spirit of neo-liberalism. 'The neo-liberal economic model Lacayo espouses, while making some accommodation to Sandinista demands, has whittled away at the transformations of the 1980s – in health, agriculture, education, industry – and challenged the FSLN conception of government's relationship to the market', notes an American observer.

> Many government services have simply been withdrawn from rural areas. Other government services are becoming fee-based. Schools have been allowed to run down physically, and parents are now being asked to pay fees or volunteer to make repairs. School teachers have been laid off, and those who work do so for less than bare minimum salaries.[8]

Within the FSLN bitter disputes erupted between the leadership and its critics. In 1994 Ernesto Cardenál, Sergio Ramirez and a number of other historical Sandinista leaders were forced to quit the organization. Accusing FSLN leader Daniel

Ortega of 'Stalinist methods', Ramirez founded the small Movement for Sandinista Renovation (MRS). The Sandinistas conducted their 1996 election campaign under the slogan 'Consensus in the name of production', stressing that only nuances separated them from the candidate of the right, Arnoldo Alemán.[9] The result was a thoroughly deserved defeat for the Sandinistas and the coming to power of a new president much more reactionary than Chamorro.

The unquestionable success of the Party of Democratic Socialism in Germany in the years from 1994 to 1996 was accompanied by a sharp rise in internal discord, and by the increasingly obvious desire of a section of the party to prove its moderation. According to data from sociologists, 'the internal disputes of the PDS (especially within its leadership) have become one of the main reasons why rank and file members leave the party'.[10]

The Neurosis of the Left

One has the feeling that the left has been possessed by an instinct for suicide. The left is afraid of itself. Politicians are afraid of their own success, and instinctively or unconsciously try to thwart it or reduce it to a minimum. Since 1989 a neurosis has paralysed the left's will to struggle. Socialists do not believe the liberal theory that any form of collectivism is totalitarianism, but they suspect that this theory is true. The tragic experience of the Russian Revolution lies with a leaden weight on their consciousness. The basis of the neurosis of the left lies in a feeling of guilt for the mistakes of others, combined with a sense of powerlessness. It all comes down, in practice, to a readiness to blame yourself for everything.

Certainly the left has had reasons to blame itself. But things have changed. The left has changed, society has changed and capitalism has changed, but the left still keeps blaming itself. The time has come to cure the neurosis of the left.

The victory of capitalism in Eastern Europe, seemingly beyond dispute in the early 1990s, was beginning to arouse doubts as the decade neared its end. The West had experienced huge protest actions by workers, and in the countries of the Third World dissatisfaction with the established order had led to violence. The political left played little if any role in these processes. The crisis of the capitalist order was developing spontaneously, not in response to organized resistance by workers, and at times even despite their patience and passivity.

As a result of the victory of the West in the Cold War, Russia has been transformed into part of the periphery of the capitalist world, but there are no grounds for speaking of the birth of Russian capitalism. The regime that arose on this basis is best described by the word 'kleptocracy' – the rule of thieves. The pillage of the country went ahead in close association with the restoring of capitalist property relations and the subordination of Russia to the interests of the West. This does not at all signify that a genuine capitalism has arisen in the republics of the former Soviet Union, or that it can arise in the near future. Rather, what is involved is a peculiar symbiosis of the traditional corporative-bureaucratic order with the power of *comprador* and usurer capital. The neo-liberal reforms have led to a massive destruction of productive capacity and to the plunder of resources, but have not served to accumulate any serious national capital. The bankruptcy of capitalist modernization is even more obvious in Russia today than it was 80 years ago.

Unfortunately, it was less evident to the politicians of the left than to the mass of the population. The Communist Party of the Russian Federation (CPRF) kept its historic revolutionary name but not the commitment to anti-capitalist change. In 1993, a popular uprising in Moscow failed to bring down the reactionary government of President Yeltsin, and in 1996 the opposition failed to win the presidential election. These defeats suffered by popular and socialist forces convinced the party leadership that no radical alternative to the system was possible. Instead of presenting itself as an anti-capitalist and liberating force the party turned to nationalist rhetoric, at the same time advocating the 'consolidation' of the elites as the way out of crisis. Remaining formally in opposition, CPRF gradually became integrated into the system at the very same time as the system was falling apart.

When, in 1998–9, the system crumbled and everyone started to speak about the need for natonalization and social change most of the official left was completely unprepared.

Socialism was back in fashion. Liberal intellectuals considered themselves bound to go on record with their views on the prospects for the socialist idea, while parties calling themselves 'socialist' began to sprout like mushrooms. The Gorbachev

Foundation ideologue Yury Krasin writes that socialism is 'a vector of the development of diverse social movements gravitating toward the values of social justice'.[11] Elsewhere we read that the essence of socialism is expressed 'in the concepts of humanity, justice and integrity'.[12] Naturally, devotion to these values requires that people's political energies should be directed 'not into the channel of revolutionary radicalism, so familiar from our history but without prospects, but instead into the channel of evolutionary reformism'.[13]

According to today's way of thinking Eduard Bernstein, who considered that the end was nothing and the movement everything, was excessively radical. Bernstein believed in social change. To the intellectuals of the end of the twentieth century, socialism appears not as an alternative system to capitalism, not as a new state of social being and not even as a political movement, but as a set of values.

'Socialist Values'

In setting out to show that the political distinction between left and right retains its relevance, the Italian writer Norberto Bobbio painstakingly avoids using the very term 'socialism'. Leftists differ from rightists, in Bobbio's view, in that they profess 'the ideal of equality'.[14] In essence such a limited concept of leftism scarcely differs from its opposite. Meanwhile, the rejection of their own historical goal is becoming the political trump card through which the politicians at the head of left parties try to attract supporters. Massimo d'Alema, the leader of the Party of the Democratic Left (the former Communists) in Italy proclaims as his principle 'the abandoning of the myth of the construction of a different society'.[15] Romano Prodi, the head of the first left majority government in Italy's history was convinced that his mission consisted of implementing a whole complex of neo-liberal measures that not even the country's rightists had the resolve to carry out. With every new initiative these leaders are spitting in the faces of their own traditional supporters. Even the newspaper *La Repubblica,* which is scarcely a revolutionary publication, has described these policies of the Italian left as 'suicide'.[16]

The anti-utopian passion of the intellectuals who have 'come to see the light' has nothing in common with a turn to political realism. On the contrary, it signifies a radical break with political thinking as such. 'The possible is often achieved', Max Weber wrote, 'only because an attempt was made to go beyond its bounds and to penetrate the realm of the impossible'.[17] The strength of socialism has always consisted precisely in its ability to combine a utopian aim with a concrete programmeme of social change – to combine the goal and the movement. This is what strategy is all about. The rejection of utopianism and the replacement of the political slogan of a new social system with references to a socialist 'system of values' has to be seen as a tactful, refined form of intellectual capitulation. Making such a shift means that there is no need to struggle against capitalism or to reform it; instead, it is enough simply to live in society and to relate to events in a manner somewhat different from, say, liberals. Instead of alternative actions, we are offered the right to make critical assessments. But is this really enough to allow a significant layer of Western leftists to feel completely satisfied with life?

'Values', of course, can be thoroughly seductive. Alain Tourain and the sociologists of his school maintain that the new social movements are more radical than the old labour movement, since unlike the labour movement they are able to 'call into question the very need for modernization and progress', instead of merely calling for the redistribution of its results. Since a number of new social movements reject economic growth itself 'or simply ignore this question', they 'undermine the bases of Western rationality, at least in its most widespread variant'.[18]

Possessing 'radical values', we thus automatically become very progressive people. It is true that these values bear no relation to real life, but this is no longer important. The advantage of the historical labour movement lay in the fact that it set itself the task of forcing concrete structural changes, of altering the very way in which society was reproduced. The new radical movements, declaring the bankruptcy of the dominant principles but lacking a strategy for comprehensive structural reform, are incapable of changing anything – and are not trying. Their rise does not signify that an alternative has appeared; it is merely a symptom of spiritual crisis.

Andrey Ballaev, one of the most radical and penetrating writers for the journal *Svobodnaya mysl'* and a sort of voice of the Russian left-liberal intelligentsia of the 1990s, has observed that the left is now waging a struggle to preserve and reinforce those 'elements of socialist identity' that were accumulated in society throughout the preceding period. This cannot take the place of a radical transformation of society, but it creates an indispensable historical staging-post for such a transformation, of the kind which the bourgeoisie possessed at the beginning of its historical struggle against feudalism. Since the global transformation remains in the future, the Russian writer comes to the gloomy conclusion:

> The socialism of the present and of the immediate future is a cowardly and impoverished socialism, that smooths out the 'evil' of our social being and patches the holes in it. As such, this socialism is inevitable, deserved, necessary and tragic.[19]

But can a 'cowardly socialism' be effective? Can a policy of 'patching the holes' bring success? Great historical turns do not come all at once. They are preceded by small turns. Without radical perspectives, a firm strategy and a radical vision of the future, partial reforms are doomed. Donald Sassoon justly notes that the golden age of European socialism coincided with the most successful period in the development of capitalism. Leftists condemn bourgeois society and the thirst for profit. 'But the more successful the socialists became, the more dependent they found themselves on the prosperity of capitalism.'[20] The crises of capitalism have invariably been accompanied by severe crises of the left parties, and it has been precisely during years of economic growth that upsurges in the labour movement have been recorded. Paradoxically, it seems that what is good for capitalism is good for socialism as well. But in practice, socialist reforms have not by any means been the simple consequence of capitalist prosperity. In the 1930s and 1940s they played a decisive role in overcoming the crisis.

On the whole, the experience of Western Europe and North America confirms the neo-liberal thesis, that as a result of the implementing of broad social programmes the efficiency and competitiveness of the economy declines. Although one can cite a number of impressive exceptions, the overall picture conforms to this pattern. Nevertheless, such programmes continue to be implemented. Moreover, a clear need is felt for them. It is quite obvious that the efficiency of enterprises is not equivalent to the efficiency of the system as a whole, and that the efficiency of the economic system does not guarantee the successful development of society. In addition, contemporary capitalism has reached a state where maximizing economic efficiency (taking account of the technological, ecological, social and cultural problems that arise) leads to undermining the bases of the very society that requires maximum efficiency as a principle of its existence. The absolute, 100 per cent efficiency of all the elements of the economy would lead to the rapid collapse of the system as a whole.

The reflections of this contradiction have included the waves of social reform in the West and of the national liberation struggle in the Third World. The logic of both has been directly contrary to the logic of capitalist efficiency. The key difference between the two phenomena has been that social reform has presupposed the redistribution of wealth within society, while the national liberation movements have fought for a new relationship of forces between the countries of the centre and periphery.

On the level of ideology, this is perceived as a contradiction between efficiency and justice, or, let us say, between freedom and equality. Liberals accuse social democrats of 'inefficiency', while social democrats accuse liberals of pursuing 'anti-social policies'. Both are right. Neither can exist without the other, and however they might fight, they coexist quite well.

Defending social principles within capitalist society, social democracy acts as this society's main stabilizer. In general, modern social democracy is the embodiment of the bourgeois social principle. In this sense the continual reverses suffered by social democratic parties in the West and their constant ideological concessions to liberals, are symptoms of a new, very profound and dangerous crisis of society as a whole.

At issue here, in fact, is not an 'objective' contradiction between efficiency and justice (this is no more than words), but an inherent contradiction of the system, which can no longer reconcile the economic and social aspects of its own development and reproduction.

At one and the same time the system both 'works' (in order to be convinced of this, it is enough to go into a supermarket) and 'fails to work' (in order to see this, it can be enough to step out of the supermarket onto the street). This duality must inevitably give rise to the need for change. But what is to be changed? The logic of the bourgeois social principle suggests that the secondary elements of the system must be changed, while its bases are left intact. The trouble is that it is precisely the secondary elements of the system that work best. The source of the problems lies in the system's bases. It is these that need to be changed, as far as possible sparing the workable modern structures.

Reforms After the Revolution

If Soviet society in the late 1980s was in the dead-end of bureaucratic centralization, in the West during the same years the limited, dead-end character of the social reforms of the social democratic era was revealed as well. There too the inability of the left to suggest new alternatives meant that setbacks were inevitable. The two streams of reaction, in East and West, merged together.

In essence, what we see today is nothing other than the crisis of the historical consequences of the Russian Revolution of 1917. The social reforms of the postwar era were nothing other than a sort of reaction by Western society to this revolution. Prince Kropotkin in his time reminded Lenin that revolutionary terror held back the spread of the principles of the French Revolution in Europe for a whole 80 years. In Kropotkin's view, the same would happen with Russian socialism as well. Lenin undoubtedly took a different view. The question, of course, was not simply one of terror, but of the structures and practices to which the revolution gave issue. The Soviet model was plainly unsuitable for distribution in Europe.

The influence on Western society of the 1917 revolution was enormous, but quite different from what the ideologues of October had hoped. The Russian experience provoked concessions from the ruling classes, and at the same time became an obstacle to the search for a distinctive European model of radical change. A solution was found in reformism, and the success of the reformist efforts was in direct proportion to the seriousness of the 'revolutionary blackmail' embodied in the world communist movement and the 'Soviet menace'. This might be called a 'deferred revolution'.[21]

It is not surprising that the collapse of communism was also a catastrophe for social democracy. After 1989 the reformist course of the Western labour movement had totally exhausted itself, and there was no new ideology or strategy. The result was obvious: the West entered an epoch marked by acute social conflicts and by a lack of clear social alternatives. The place of reformism and revolutionism has been filled by a spontaneous radicalism that expresses itself in aggressive but incoherent demands and in outbursts of unorganized protest against the institutions of power.

In the early 1980s ideologues of structural reform within left social democratic currents and the ranks of the Eurocommunist parties encountered serious problems. Researchers noted that the left was torn between believing that '"alternative programmes" based on "mixed economies" or market socialism' could work, and recognizing that if capitalist classes did tolerate these reforms, the reforms would not be socialist.[22] This contradiction cannot be resolved on the theoretical plane. The dynamic of the development of capitalism is such that the system cannot stabilize itself without making use of resources and institutions from outside.

Market capitalism is a system that subordinates the process of production to the process of exchange. From the point of view of liberal theory it is precisely exchange that will become the central and main function of economic life. From the point of view of history and of normal logic this is clearly absurd. In the past, when new commodities did not appear so often, it was still possible to suppose that demand gave rise to supply. But the 1980s showed in exquisite fashion how the development and mass production of commodities of a new type (video recorders, personal computers, microwave ovens and so forth) also gave birth to massive demand for them. However, the absurdity of liberal theory is psychologically quite acceptable from the point of view of everyday life. The times of natural economy, when people produced goods for their own needs, are long past. Under capitalism production is pointless unless it is oriented toward exchange. But for people it is quite natural to confuse the purpose of their actions with their causes.

A system which reduces primary functions to secondary ones, restricting all the wealth of human possibilities to the narrow tasks of *homo economicus*, inevitably creates unbearable stresses within itself. It constantly undermines its own potential for reproduction. The great secret of the capitalist system is that, unlike traditional societies, it is not self-sufficient. This is also one of the reasons for the astonishing dynamism of the capitalist economy. In order not to perish, it has to go forward. Growth makes it possible to remove or to soften contradictions that would otherwise tear capitalist society apart from within. The economy has to develop, or it will collapse. However, permanent growth is impossible, especially since it is prevented by the contradictions of the system itself.

A pure, complete capitalism would soon reach the point of self-destruction. This is why capitalism, from its early stages of development, has always needed external stabilizers. Rosa Luxemburg showed the importance for maintaining the equilibrium of capitalism of the role played by the incorporation into the world system of the non-capitalist periphery, where a fully formed bourgeois society has not come into being. In the countries of the centre, the institutions and traditions that remain as the heritage of feudalism have played a no less important role. Monarchy, the bourgeoisified British aristocracy, academic establishments, the Christian religion and the Confucian 'family' in the East have not merely been the heritage of the past, but also a guarantee of future stability.

Will Hutton has an excellent sense for the degree to which the bourgeois order depends on traditional institutions:

> Capitalism requires the profit motive and a go-getting individualism if it is to function, but it also takes place within inherited social and political boundaries. It is not just that capitalism needs rules to function effectively; the firms that are its life-blood are social as well as economic organisations. They are formed by human beings with human as well as contractual claims upon each other, and behind this social world lies the moral domain. Unless this is recognised economic performance is likely to be unsatisfactory.[23]

The protestant ethic as well was not merely an ideological spur to personal success; in no less a degree, it was 'a source of cooperative economic strength'. In the development of capitalism on the European continent, pre-bourgeois traditions also played a huge role:

> From the Prussian tradition comes a sense of the need for discipline and for a regulated order in human affairs; from Catholicism the tradition of social solidarity and 'subsidiarity'

– the location of decision making as close as possible to those who are affected by it.[24]

The strength of the protestant ethic lay in the fact that while being bourgeois, it was at the same time also traditional. But as modernization proceeded, the old institutions became weakened or bourgeoisified to the point where they could no longer play their compensatory role effectively. Their place was gradually taken by the labour movement. The potential grave-diggers of capitalism acted simultaneously as its support. Capitalism found new props not in institutions inherited from the past, but in newly conceived elements of the future: the welfare state, social democracy and the New Deal.[25]

Needing reforms, capitalism at the same time is constantly forced to restrain them in order to stop the process from going beyond the bounds of the permissible, and is also forced to annul the results of these reforms whenever the direct need for them disappears. The neo-liberal wave testifies not only to the fact that social democratic reforms did not succeed in altering capitalism fundamentally, and in the final accounting were defeated by it, but also to the fact that these reforms included a definite (though generally unrealized) potential for systemic changes. It was precisely for this reason that many institutions of the welfare state were demolished.

The New Realism

The crisis of the left in the 1990s obliged many politicians and ideologues to rethink the role of the labour movement under the conditions of capitalism. Earlier, the stabilizing role played by socialism in relation to capitalism had either been denied or attributed to the unprincipled actions of social traitors, to the need for temporary, transitional measures and so forth. Now, playing this stabilizing role is seen as the key task of the left and as its main strength.

The historian of socialism Donald Sassoon is convinced that the leaders of social democratic parties who accept the need for privatization and the free market are not time-servers and political renegades but sages who have realized the true meaning of history. It remains only to reject the idea that socialism 'is a state of affairs which is to occur after capitalism'. Instead, we are urged to recognize that 'the object of socialism is not the abolition of capitalism but its coexistence with social justice'.[26]

Because the idea of justice is not rejected by rightists, and because the need to improve the system is recognized by the ruling class, the left therefore should not struggle against the bourgeoisie and the right-wing parties, but collaborate with them. But if leftists do not differ qualitatively from rightists, why are they needed at all? The evolutionary improvement of capitalism is fundamentally incompatible with reformism. Evolution demands not social reformers but thoughtful conservatives, competently carrying on day-to-day administration. Reform is needed where natural evolution, improving the structures and making routine adjustments of course, is insufficient; where contradictions fraught with ever more serious crises are accumulating. A reformist movement begins by stating that the system is bad. It is something quite different that the reformers are not intent on demolishing the system 'down to its foundations', but merely wish to replace important elements of it. A sharp critique of capitalism formed the starting point not only for revolutionary Marxism, but also for social democratic 'revisionism'. That is why social democrats succeeded in carrying out reforms in the 1940s and 1950s. Roosevelt's New Deal in the US also proceeded from the premise that the system needed to be altered, that society was in a profound crisis and that a social explosion could be avoided only if serious changes were put in place. The 'new realism' in Europe, by contrast, proceeds from approval and acceptance of the present society. The question is not whether this society is good or bad in itself (it is good for some, and for others – not so good). The problem is that no alternatives are being developed on this basis.

Socialism has managed to play a major role in improving capitalism precisely because of its anti-capitalist essence. If socialism were not a real alternative, if it did not have its own economic and social logic, on the basis of which creating a new society was a real possibility, it would not have been able to develop ideas and approaches useful for the successful introduction of change. Reforming the system required an ideological impulse from outside. If socialist society ceased to be a fundamental alternative to capitalism, if the labour movement lost its capacity for aggressive behaviour and became incapable of determined struggle against the bourgeoisie, it would not be able to curb anyone or anything. Without class hatred there would not be any social reforms or social partnership. As a rule, partnership is not born of mutual sympathies between the partners, but of an understanding that refusing to collaborate could have catastrophic results.

The main ace up the sleeve of the new realism, according to its ideologues, is the ability of people equipped with such ideas to attain power. Here is the essence of the political culture thanks to which Tony Blair appeared at the head of the Labour Party. 'The long period in opposition had united the party round a single objective: to regain power at virtually any cost', Sassoon notes.[27] The aim, of course, is a worthy one, but what happens next? This is unclear even to many adherents of the new realism. 'To know that it is necessary to innovate, without knowing how to do it or in which direction to proceed, is not necessarily an intellectually vacuous position to hold', the British historian declares.[28] Nevertheless he does not doubt for a minute that the chosen course is correct, wherever it might lead.

The book, *The State We're In*, by Will Hutton (who was called 'Blair's guru' in the British press) has in practice become the first attempt to formulate a positive, more or less systematic new realist programme, and to show that there are fundamental differences between new realism and neo-liberalism. Accepting the bourgeois order, Hutton insists that within the framework of this system there are various models – 'rival capitalisms', as it were.[29] His sympathies are totally on the side of the German model. This is a capitalism that assumes social partnership, regulation and responsibility to society.

> The Germans have two key mechanisms. First they exploit the stakeholder culture engendered by cooperative capitalism to lower the cost of capital for all enterprises, banks included. Shares are regarded as tokens of a long-term relationship rather than a trading asset, so that dividend payments can be lower and payback periods lengthened. Second, public banks at both state and regional level are constrained in their dividend distributions; profits build up as reserves and balance sheets are strengthened which gives a stable platform from which to lend longterm at keen rates of interest.[30]

This system ensures steady development of the economy, low unemployment and mutual understanding between workers and employers. In short, Germany as described by Hutton recalls a sort of capitalist 'city of the Sun', a trouble-free community of blameless citizens.

The irony of the situation lies in the fact that while the British admirers of the 'German model' have been in raptures over its virtues, in Germany itself people have been speaking of the system's obvious crisis. Unemployment has risen sharply in the course of the 1990s, and the gap between the eastern and western parts of the country has not only persisted, but has taken on a structural character; the 'new lands' have been transformed into an internal periphery. The government of Helmut Kohl has been gradually dismantling the system of social welfare (*Sozialabbau*). Explaining the reasons for the dramatic rise in the popularity of the Party of Democratic Socialism (PDS), one of the party's founders, Hans Modrow, has said that amid the crisis of the German model of the social state, 'the need is again being felt for left reformist ideas'.[31] The leader of the parliamentary group of the PDS, Gregor Gysi, has written that this is quite natural in a society where 'the number of poor is growing in direct proportion to the number of millionaires, and the social welfare system is being radically curtailed because of the growth of indebtedness'.[32]

Not only did the 'German model' described in Hutton's book not exist in the 1990s, but in the form the British writer depicts it, it never has existed anywhere (just as the mythical Europe of which Russian Westernizers have always dreamt never has been and never could be). However, Hutton's programme is not reducible to a naively utopian appeal to transform the real Britain into a fairy-tale Germany. Hutton proposes a broad list of 'feasible and achievable reforms':

> A written constitution; the democratisation of civil society; the republicanisation of finance; the recognition that the market economy has to be managed and regulated, both at home and abroad; the upholding of a welfare state that incorporates social citizenship; the construction of a stable international financial order beyond the nation state.[33]

If we add to this appeals to nationalize natural monopolies and to campaign for a more regulated international capitalism, the programme of reforms appears genuinely impressive. If Tony Blair were to carry it out, he would undoubtedly be the most radical social democratic leader of the past decade. But there is no need to criticize Blair for indecisiveness; such a programme cannot be implemented in any case.

It is significant that in providing a historical foundation for the new realism, Donald Sassoon points to the Spanish and French socialists as examples. Meanwhile 'Blair's guru' Will Hutton comments in extremely negative terms on their actions while in power – actions which for practical purposes did not differ from the policies of the neo-liberals.[34] This contradiction is entirely natural. As an ideologue, Hutton is obliged to single out those elements of the new realism that distinguish it from the prevailing neo-liberal doctrines. But it is precisely this distinction that cannot be observed in practice. Left-wing economists constantly criticize their liberal colleagues for regarding society as a soulless mechanism, ignoring the social and cultural aspects of the processes that are occurring. Then, when they set about formulating their own positive programmes, they fall into the same error. An 'optimal' economic policy is impossible because every social group, whatever it proclaims, strives not for ideal equilibrium, or maximum efficiency, or even for the triumph of justice, but for concrete results for itself. Equilibrium does not appear where 'optimal' economic theories are employed, but where a balance is established between contending forces.

A real ruling class will actively resist any attempts at reform. Even if these reforms are essential for the overall interests of capitalism, any interest group that does not directly benefit from them will do everything it can to thwart them. The counterweight to sabotage by the elites has always been the mobilization of the masses. But this is the last thing that enters into the plans of the new realists.

The Dialectic of Reform

By the early twentieth century social democracy had begun to display a duality of theory and practice. On the one hand was reformist practice, and on the other was the socialist utopia. But the one did not simply contradict the other; it also complemented it. Moderate reforms and optimum decisions have never inspired anyone to struggle. It was precisely for this reason that the social democrats for so long maintained their official allegiance to the socialist ideal that they were in no particular hurry to attain. Under the new conditions, when belief in utopia has been buried and the Soviet threat does not exist, the reformers are unable to mobilize either supporters or arguments in order to frighten their opponents. The forces of capital that confront the demobilized workers are organized and united by the neo-liberal hegemony. Unless this relationship of forces changes, reforms are impossible.

The result, as one of the leaders of the Brazilian Workers' Party justly remarked, is that:

> a moderate but consistent progressive today cannot be other than radical. The scenario, simplified to a certain degree, is as follows: on the one side are the big capitalists, the partisans of the market and the postmodernists, while on the other are the people who maintain a sense of solidarity and dignity.[35]

At a certain point any reformist project faces a choice between radicalization and retreat. In the late twentieth century this choice typically comes on to the agenda at a very early stage, almost before real reforms have even begun. One cannot 'concede what is secondary, in order to retain what is most important', because there will be nothing left. The logic of the new realism guarantees that the choice will be made in favour of rejecting reforms entirely.

Nor does a policy of concessions guarantee the friendship of the ruling class. The theory that electoral success depends on the ability of politicians to sacrifice their own principles is, to put it mildly, questionable. 'The plain fact is that policies of accommodation have not been successful in electoral terms', the publication *Socialist Campaign Group News*, issued by leftists within the British parliamentary Labour Party, noted in January 1997.

> In contrast, the outstanding electoral victories of the left in the last twenty-five years have been won on radical programmes. This was the case when Mitterand was elected the first time in France, when socialists were first elected in Spain, and when

> Papandreou was first elected in Greece. In Britain too, the last Labour victory in 1974 was secured on a progressive programme. None of these governments eventually fulfilled their early promise, but this does not affect the conclusion that their initial radical programmes appealed to the electorate.[36]

It is by no means true that radicalism must lead to victory, but cowardice and a lack of principles are even less a guarantee of electoral success. The political theory of the new realists holds that winning seats, not to mention winning parliamentary majorities, amounts in itself to an achievement. Here we find the main philosophical and political underpinnings of the new realist current: winning elections, coming to power and obtaining government portfolios comprise the whole sense and purpose of political activity. Power is no longer a means, but becomes an end in itself, an ultimate value. There is nothing Nietzschean about this. To brand such an approach as totalitarian would be unjust, since in this case the notion of power involved is very modest. By power here is understood not the ability to act, direct and transform – the ability valued so much by all the great reformers, liberators, heroes and tyrants – but the simple and peaceful state of being in office. Before us we find the quintessential world-view of the functionary in the conditions of modern Western democracy. The art of politics consists of maximizing the number of portfolios and posts held by one's own group. Democracy consists of the competition of various groups for a limited number of seats.

Lessons from Eastern Europe

The political successes of new realism in this field are indisputable, but there is a problem here as well. The faster the new realists come to power, the faster they lose it. Still worse, once they have lost power they will most likely be unable to win it again. The Spanish Socialist Party, unquestionably a model for Sassoon and for politicians like Blair, has already lost power. In Lithuania the Democratic Labour Party was the first left party in Eastern Europe to come to power with the goal of implementing a right-wing programme. Its success marked the onset of a 'left' wave in the region. The return of the right began in Lithuania as well. The catastrophic defeat suffered by the Democratic Labour Party in the 1996 parliamentary elections was the entirely natural consequence of its rule.

In 1993 and 1994 'realistic' leftists came to power almost everywhere in Eastern Europe, promising not the defence of the interests of the working class but 'honest, competent and responsible government', and privatization that would take into account 'the interests of the collective'. These were very modern leftists, sure that neo-liberal reform was 'an essential condition for overcoming extremely acute social problems and for redistributing the national income in favour of workers'.[37]

In Bulgaria the government of 'left realists' collapsed in 1997 under the pressure of massive outbursts of protest. Unlike their colleagues in other Eastern European countries, the Bulgarian socialists made an honest effort to fulfil their social obligations, while at the same time pressing ahead with the privatization policy begun by the right and conscientiously making payments on the country's debts to Western creditors. The consequence was a rapid increase in inflation and a fall in living standards. While annual inflation ran at 300 per cent, wages merely doubled. The result was the defeat of the socialists in the elections and an outbreak of mass disturbances. The sum total of the economic wisdom of the people who then came to power was expressed in the words of the representative of the European Bank for Reconstruction and Development in the countries of Southern Europe: 'The key words for the success of the Bulgarian economy are to make it private, private, private.'[38]

The brilliant success of the new realism in Britain, where supporters of the doctrine first won a majority in the Labour Party and then in 1997 led it to power, was perceived by many as the harbinger of a new crisis. 'The very speed with which it achieved its dominance testifies to the shallowness of its roots', one left-wing commentator observed.[39] New Labour arose not as the outcome of a long and complex process of rethinking strategy, but as a consequence of the demoralization of the left movement and of media manipulation. Its destructive consequences have been enormous, and it would be naive to think that after the crash of the new realism it will be possible to restore the ideological and moral status quo ante.

The Case of South Africa

The tragedy is that those who come to power only to find themselves in the trap of the new realism include not only *nomenklatura* 'leftists' in Eastern Europe and unprincipled political careerists in the West, but also real revolutionaries in South Africa. Proclaiming a radical reorientation of the economy in the interests of the oppressed majority, the African National Congress government, with the active participation of representatives of the Communist Party and the trade unions, began in 1995 and 1996 to put a consistent neo-liberal programme into practice.

Immediately after coming to power in 1994, the African National Congress adopted its Reconstruction and Development Programme (RDP). The document appeared very radical, orienting the government toward 'meeting basic needs', 'developing our human resources', 'democratizing the state and society' and so forth. It began with a preface by Nelson Mandela, who declared that unless the social problems afflicting the bulk of the population were solved, democracy would have little content and would be short-lived. At the heart of the programme were six basic principles. The programme had to be 'integrated and sustainable' and 'people-driven'; it had to 'link reconstruction and development', and to guarantee 'peace and security for all', 'nation-building' and 'democratization'.[40] The popular character of the reforms that were carried out had to be ensured 'by encouraging broader participation in decisions about the economy in both the private and public sectors'.[41] What was lacking from the programme was any hint at the clear interconnection between the development of the public sector and the satisfying of basic needs. Without this, the programme was transformed into an impressively complete and systematic catalogue of the good wishes of a government sympathetic to the people. There is no doubting the sincerity of the people who framed it, but proclaiming such humane goals has not by itself improved people's lives.

It is significant that this programme, drawn up by the African National Congress with the participation of the communists, has not aroused any particular objections among conservatives. National Party leader de Klerk voiced support for it, adding: 'We must at all costs guard against a divisive political philosophy entering the RDP. It must not be socialist or capitalist. It must work for the people.'[42] This 'ideologically neutral' programme was not only inoffensive to the old elite, but also quite impossible to fulfil, since without a definite political philosophy there can be neither firm decisions nor a clear choice of methods.

The Communist Party tried to defend the RDP as a 'people-driven process', declaring that the programme's key aspect was its commitment to 'restructuring and redistribution', which were said to 'necessarily imply struggle'.[43] However, the country's transitional constitution blocked any possibility of using expropriation as a method of redistribution, while the government's policies did not provide for an expansion of the state sector or of public services, which could have served the same ends.

A certain number of Communist Party activists realized that more radical measures were required. These people envisaged the 'decommodification of basic needs', and called for 'struggles to transform market power relations'. Ultimately, a new hegemonic project was seen as necessary.[44] But by this time the Communist Party itself had been deeply divided and to a significant degree paralysed by the struggle between radicals and the realists who had taken on the role of champions of neo-liberal hegemony within the liberation movement.

The practical measures that were taken to implement the Reconstruction and Development Programme were quite unlike what the ideologues had promised. The government set out to privatize the state sector and to 'restrain' wages. The champions of these policies were not right-wing conservatives, not representatives of the privileged white elite, but leading figures within the ANC – Vice-President Thabo Mbeki and Minister of Finances Trevor Manuel.

Government representatives declared that privatization was absolutely necessary to improve the lives of the people, since it would strengthen the confidence of investors, call forth a stream of capital investment and, through raising efficiency, stimulate economic growth. The press described this strategy as 'cautious Thatcherism'.[45] The only way in which the representatives of the ANC differed from neo-liberal economists was in the constant stress they placed on the need for a social partnership that would see business and labour 'marching in tandem, hand in hand together, to build our nation'. The two sides were called upon to 'pursue the long-term national interest' in the knowledge that some of the policies might 'in the short term negatively affect our constituencies'.[46]

This could not fail to arouse confusion and argument among leftists. On the whole, supporters of social democratic ideas were prepared to reconcile themselves to such a change of course on the condition that it was implemented with the agreement and participation of workers themselves. In this Dr Eddie Webster saw a peculiarity of the South African situation. The ANC government was practising a 'multi-layered institutionalized negotiation process between classes', he noted. 'These tripartite and bipartite arrangements', he maintained, 'are not part of neo-liberalism, indeed they are a creative challenge to the global agenda of neo-liberalism'.[47] The institutionalized representation of workers really is a major achievement of social democracy. But what is of decisive importance is not the fact that these institutions exist, but the content of their activity. If they are used in order to bind workers to a neo-liberal project, they become transformed into weapons of self-exploitation, and their role becomes profoundly reactionary. This was pointed out by the trade union ideologue Oupa Lehulere, replying to Eddie Webster. The binding of the left forces and of the COSATU trade unions to the neo-liberal project has paralysed their capacity for resistance. The dominant position among leftists is becoming 'the embracing of the politics of the neo-liberal right by omission and by keeping silent'.[48]

In the view of the trade unions, by contrast, the policy of privatization raised doubts about the readiness of the authorities to conduct reforms in the interests of workers. Economists close to COSATU insisted that instead of being privatized, the public sector should be reconstructed 'to meet the needs of the majority', with innovations including the devolution of management responsibility and an increase in management accountability. A new type of administration had to be created through decentralization and democratization. 'Structures and decision-making processes which are open to public scrutiny and which are accountable to society (which consumes public services) and to public sector workers need to be set up, including at the parliamentary level.'[49] Since privatization was being carried out in pursuit of goals directly counterposed to this, the trade union leaders decisively rejected it. 'We view privatization as one of the major threats to the vision of a better life for all', declared the COSATU leadership.[50] The words were followed by action. Protests organized by the trade unions seriously delayed and in part blocked the implementation of the government's programme. However, the ability of the trade unions and the left to resist the government's plans effectively was seriously weakened by their unwillingness to rock the boat and to undermine 'their own power'. In this respect, 'leftists' pursuing right-wing policies are better partners, tactically, for the bourgeoisie than traditional right-wingers.

The moral and political basis for this policy is becoming the desire not to rock the boat as the process of democratic change goes ahead. But even if we accept the correctness of this approach, it does not by any means follow that leftists have to accept responsibility for social and economic policies that cut across the interests of workers. Opposition to the government elected by the majority is not in any way equal to an attempt to destabilize democracy.

'The situation of the South African Communist Party at the end of apartheid rule was in some senses reminiscent of that of the French or Italian CPs at the time of the liberation', notes the British historian Willie Thompson. As a result the party 'finds itself out of its own experience doing much the same kind of thing that its French and Italian counterparts did at Stalin's command'.[51] However, such a comparison is lame in both legs. In postwar Western Europe the communists who came to power as part of the coalitions of the resistance were not a revolutionary force, but they had genuine reformist perspectives. Thompson himself acknowledges that at that time ideas of social progress were dominant. Not even the Cold War that began in the late 1940s could prevent this. As the ruling elites strove to retain their control over society, they were themselves forced to implement reforms in line with the general thrust of left ideology, carrying out, to use Gramsci's words, a 'passive revolution'. By contrast, the leftists who have come to power in the 1990s are dealing with the global hegemony of neoliberalism, and the result is that for practical purposes they have lost their reformist perspectives. Transforming these perspectives into reality would be impossible without entering into a bitter conflict with the ruling elites, both on a national and on a global level.

The progressive goals of RDP were abandoned one by one and new priorities were formulated in the government's macroeconomic Growth, Employment and Redistribution policy

(GEAR). It was publicly presented in June 1996. The process leading up to its 'adoption' consisted of a small team of 'experts' put together under the aegis of the Department of Trade and Industry and the Department of Finance. It was then presented to the Cabinet (without any prior consultation outside of the government), accepted and finally unveiled to the public as the new macro-economic policy. This policy was clearly based on a monetarist approach and provoked confrontation with the trade unions. While South African socialists, communists and trade union leaders have been pondering whether the time has come to cross over into opposition, and asking themselves whether the masses would understand such a move, the workers themselves have been expressing more and more open dissatisfaction with the measures of 'their' government. Privatization and austerity were first met with strikes, and then with mass disturbances. The government in turn switched relatively quickly from exhortations to the use of force. In February 1997, when protest demonstrations began in 'coloured' townships in the Johannesburg area, the police opened fire. Leftists throughout the world, raised in the tradition of solidarity with the ANC's struggle for the rights or the majority, were shocked:

> Television viewers around the world on February 6 may have thought they had accidentally tuned into a program of archival footage from South Africa's apartheid days: florid, bull-necked cops hidden behind menacing yellow armored 'hippos' unloading volley after volley of tear gas, rubber bullets, birdshot and 'sharp' ammunition into crowds of protesting township residents; and scenes of dead and wounded South Africans. Sadly, it was not a documentary but that day's events in the 'new' South Africa.[52]

In April 1995 a national congress of the South African Communist Party approved a set of Strategic Perspectives, in which the need was stressed for radical measures to transform society. This document accurately reflected the state of contemporary Marxist thought, and can be counted among the best programmatic texts adopted by left parties during the 1990s. It called for the creating of a modern decentralized public sector, and for the democratization of the economy. Criticizing the defeatist illusions of those who considered that globalization had made radical policies impossible, the authors of the document emphasized that on coming to power, leftists through their own actions had to create a 'new global situation'. For this, collaboration between the countries of the South and international solidarity of progressive forces were essential.[53]

However, this excellent document not only failed to help the Communist Party in its struggle against the growing neo-liberal influences within the government, but was not even able to stop communist ministers from implementing neo-liberal policies. The trouble was that globalization and the neo-liberal onslaught were perceived as purely external phenomena, while the analysis of South African society itself remained completely traditional. While indicating that the bourgeoisie was still 'the main strategic opponent', the party ideologues pointed to substantial contradictions within its ranks: 'There are important tensions between the foreign multinationals, local monopoly capital, and the non-monopoly sector.'[54]

Attempts to split the bourgeoisie along the lines of these contradictions were naive precisely because they failed to take account of the new global reality. In fact, globalization is by no means an external factor. Its most important aspect is the hegemony of neo-liberal ideology in relation to the entire bourgeois class. Whatever the contradictions and differences, the main mass of capital follows its vanguard, since it does not have any obvious alternative. In the same way, the ideologues of the South African Communist Party did not take into account the stratification occurring within the progressive movement itself, or the influence on the movement of neo-liberalism as a dominant ideology against which it was necessary to wage a struggle within one's own ranks.

Within the framework of the neo-liberal hegemonic project, the abolition of apartheid was essential for the further consolidation of the bourgeoisie, for overcoming the rift between black and white business, and for the integration of the rising black middle layers and bureaucracy. Hence the main strategic problem has not been external influences, but the entirely natural inclusion of part of the national liberation movement in the neo-liberal project. The dividing line is not between communists and non-communists, but between the people who consider that their main goal is to reassure investors and those who, as before, defend the interests of workers.

A strategy of splitting the bourgeoisie would have real prospects for success only if it were combined with an offensive aimed at radically transforming the structure of society. Such a policy would create new, concrete alternatives, and would confront the captains of business with new dilemmas to which they lacked ready answers. However, the demand for 'political realism' is tantamount to a ban on social experimentation. Political realism has thus doomed the left to passively playing the role assigned to it in the neo-liberal scenario.

Analysing the South African Communist Party's document on the pages of an American Marxist journal, Peter Marcuse notes: 'No concrete radical proposals are put forward that would move the country in the direction of socialism; no radical critique of government policy is suggested, no alternate program put forward.' Everything is reduced to an effort to push the ANC government to the left – which in practice means trying to halt its drift to the right. But the party's document does not pose the question of how to fight for this goal, from within the coalition or through leaving it. It is far from obvious that a break with the government would represent the best possible decision. But disturbingly, the party's strategic document 'is silent on this, the big question of strategy'.[55] This means that the party leadership prefers to drift with the current.

The Rise of the Militant Right

Instead of waging a principled struggle against neo-liberalism, leftists are preferring to call for its 'softening'. Simon Clarke has noted ironically that the new realism is 'monetarism tempered by humanity'.[56] One of the leaders of the Polish Social Democrats (the 'renovated' Communist Party) set out the formula of the new realism still more bluntly: 'My attachment to the left really means that I don't think you should take away all the elements of social protection from people at the same time. That can be done gradually; people have to get used to it.'[57]

The monetarist, neo-liberal economic philosophy is inhumane in its very essence. Therefore, the 'humanization' of monetarism makes it contradictory, inconsistent and largely unsuccessful. The new realism of the left is not only a humanized neo-liberalism, but also an ineffective one. The triumph of New Labour at the elections on 1 May 1997, like the earlier successes of the left-centrist bloc in Italy and the victories of post-communist parties in Lithuania, Poland, Hungary and so forth, provided striking proof of the fact that the new realism has been an effective means of bidding for power. But the majority of voters in all the cases noted above voted in essence not for the policies urged by the left, and not even against the politicians of the right, but above all for change. And change is what the new realism cannot offer and is unwilling to offer. The very point of the new realism lies in its continuity with relation to the defeated rightists. The more hopes the victory of such leftists arouse, the deeper and more dramatic will be the eventual disappointment.

New realists come to power only where the right-wing parties are so weakened and discredited that they cannot hold onto office. In Spain after decades of right-wing dictatorship, the conservative politicians were so compromised that they could simply not compete with the socialists, especially since the bourgeoisie had nothing against a 'left-wing government' that was implementing right-wing policies. But as soon as a change of generations took place, and new people without ties to the past appeared among the rightists, the socialists lost power. The usual pattern is that the socialists come to power on a wave of universal irritation with neo-liberal policies, and then after their victory continue putting these policies into practice. The inevitable result is that the socialists lose their authority and are defeated. Meanwhile, the downfall of the left realists does not necessarily result in moderate right-wingers returning to power. The presence in office of 'realistic' leftists is everywhere accompanied by a rapid growth in the ranks of the radical anti-democratic right. In Britain, where the left was out of power for many years, there are relatively few neo-fascists. But in France, the abrupt rise of Le Pen has been one of the most obvious consequences of 14 years of socialist rule. In Hungary, where social-democratized communists came to power in 1994 as exemplary new realists, the situation developed in even more dramatic fashion. The renovated Socialist Party that returned to office in 1994 has turned out to bear little resemblance either to the old communist structure, or to a traditional workers' organization. Representatives of the former *nomenklatura* no longer play a key role within it, while the *nomenklatura* itself has undergone dramatic changes and has been definitively bourgeoisified. 'The number of women and young people – and of enterprise directors – testifies to the way the party has been renewed with relation to its ancestor', sociologists note:

> And since its worker base is more and more losing hope, the party's future rests on its ability to anchor itself in intermediate classes that in political terms are extremely volatile. Unless they possess true political fibre, the more calculating members of the old *nomenklatura* will therefore hesitate to trust in the party to guarantee the privileges they have acquired. Where this is concerned, the prime question which is now posed is that of the strengthening of political power in the face of pressures from economic lobbies. In this sense, the situation in Hungary is close to that in France.

What is involved here is a clear gap between the activity of the 'political class' and the concerns of ordinary people.

> In a period when the rich are growing richer at an accelerated rate while the very poor are becoming more and more numerous, the fate of democracy depends largely on the confidence which the population are prepared to place in the political class.[58]

The continued implementation by the left of neo-liberal policies has made the government unpopular. 'Traditional left demands are being appropriated by the far right and mixed with racism and nationalism, which is a disastrous combination for Hungary', observes the ideologue of the party's 'Left Platform' faction, Tamas Krausz. New rightists who enjoy support from the dispossessed sector of the population present 'a far worse prospect than the first conservative government'.[59] In the 1998 elections while Socialists lost power and the 'respectable' right won, the far-right Hungarian Justice and Life Party headed by Istvan Czurka for the first time managed to get seats in the parliament. During this election, as liberal commentator Miklos Harasti writes, 'the right–left divide seemed to be nothing more than a cultural distinction. National orientation signifies right, and internationalist, or cosmopolitic, if you wish, means left.' However, the same Harasti acknowledged that Socialists carried out privatization and austerity while the right in Hungary defended the remaining elements of the welfare system, fought against the introduction of university tuition payments, etc. 'The right ... campaigned like class-warfare fighters against the influence of "bankers" and "foreign capitalists". It was the left which based its propaganda on traditional capitalist "values".'[60]

The Elitist Left

The realists are least of all interested in their traditional social base. They are sure that the majority of the poor and the working class will support them in any case, since these social layers have nowhere else to go. The politics of the new realists are oriented toward winning the support of the middle layers. But the poor, forgotten by everyone, are unexpectedly finding an alternative. The obvious and quite open betrayal of their interests by the 'left' forces them to turn to extreme rightists, who not only make demagogic use of the hardships of the poor, but unlike the 'realistic' leftists really do put forward demands that reflect the concrete interests of a significant part of the population.[60]

The masses, unlike the political parties, reject the arguments of propagandistic 'good sense' if their own experience contradicts this trite wisdom. Daniel Singer has expressed this mood as follows: 'To hell with your propaganda – if this is the future you are offering us and our children, we don't want it!'[61] For the first time since the Second World War the extreme rightists, who under the conditions of neo-liberal hegemony have preserved a sort of ideological immunity, and who unlike the left are untouched by any moral crisis and do not suffer from political neuroses, may be about to become a real popular force in Europe. In their speeches, just demands are mixed with nationalist and racist lies to the effect that immigrants and people of other nationalities are the source of all evil. But unless we recognize that, for example, the hostility of the new right to European integration corresponds fully to the moods and needs of millions of people, we will not understand the reasons for the swift rise in support for politicians such as Le Pen. The 'leftists' say that everything is fine, the rightists deny it, and simple people know perfectly well who it is that in this case is lying. The 'leftists' say there is no alternative to people tightening their belts and going into a United Europe, while the ordinary French, British and even German citizen often has no wish to go there, let alone with a tightened belt. Sociologists consider that if a referendum had been held in Britain late in 1996 on the question of relations with the rest of Europe, the supporters of integration would have lost.[62] In this respect it is right-wing Tories who most accurately reflect the moods of the ordinary voter. The coming to power of the 'left' allows conservatives, freed from the burden of government responsibility and from old obligations, to shift further to the right – and to find broad support for this from the popular masses.

In the mid-1990s, the extreme right in general showed far more sensitivity to the moods of the masses than the moderate left or the respectable centre-right. It is significant that, after the mass protests by French workers in 1995, the National Front sharply altered its rhetoric. Instead of criticizing state sector workers, who had been characterized as 'privileged functionaries', the nationalist leaders began speaking of workers' just demands, and even began setting up their own trade unions, arguing that they alone were prepared seriously to defend the interests of French workers against globalization.[63]

Tobias Abse, analysing the victory of the left bloc in Italy, notes that an important element among the supporters of the Italian left 'still see it as the bearer of a tradition of social reform'.[64] It is not hard to guess how disappointed these loyal and disciplined left voters became when they encountered the practices of new realism. The failures of the left government created a fertile milieu for the growth of right-wing populism. In Italy, however, there was also a radical left alternative in the form of Rifondazione Communista. The situation was quite different in countries where such an alternative was weak or non-existent.

Something similar occurred in Poland, where in 1997 it was the extreme right, acting through the trade union Solidarnosc, that raised the banner of resistance to the programme of market reforms being implemented by the former communists. The Union of Labour (Unia Pracy – UP), which was criticizing the government from the left, did not have the same mass social base and strong position in the trade unions as the right. 'There is a certain schizophrenia in UP's programme,' notes the British journal *Labour Focus on Eastern Europe*, 'between its categorical commitment to the imperatives of the market – its programme intones the familiar mantra "there is no alternative" – and its commitments to the trade unions and enhanced social rights'. Despite the UP's clear radicalism on many questions, ambivalence constantly arose 'as to whether its identity was to be liberal or social-democratic'.[65]

Vacillating between a desire to resist the neo-liberal course and readiness to defend the authorities against attacks from the right, the Union of Labour could not in principle become an organizing centre for mass discontent. The same contradictions also characterized the more radical Socialist Party (PPS). It too was afraid of destabilizing the 'left-wing' post-communist government. At the same time, it declared its fidelity to 'Western values' and its desire to see Poland join NATO and the European Union, ignoring the question of the social nature of these organizations.

During the period when there was no left alternative, liberals and opposition socialists found themselves in a common trap. Karol Modzelewski, a former dissident and Solidarnosc ideologue who later became a leader of the Union of Labour, stated gloomily that liberal politicians were mistaken when they rejoiced at the failures of the post-communist parties in Eastern Europe. When the left was totally discredited, mass worker protests that had been called to condemn sackings, and that combined anti-communist slogans with anti-market demands, would provide fertile soil for the growth of nationalist and populist organizations. 'The fall of the post-communists amid the fires of social conflict will not lead to the return to power of right-wing liberals', he predicted. The crisis of the new realism was aiding the rise of a far more reactionary and aggressive opposition.[66]

An analogous situation arose in Hungary in the mid-1990s after the post-communist Socialists came to power. Large numbers of party activists remarked with horror that 'their' government had turned out to be hostile to them. As a result the party's Left Platform faction, acting in open opposition to the government's policies, grew rapidly in strength. 'The uncritical service of foreign and domestic capital is depriving the socialist left of its future', a document of the oppositionists stated. 'With such a trajectory, the existence of the party will merely be an episode in the pitiful story of the restoration of capitalism in Hungary.'[67] Worse still, the right-wing course of the left-wing government was opening the road to power for much more reactionary forces. 'There is the danger that rising nationalist populism could sweep away a discredited left.'[68]

As the left turns elitist, the right becomes populist. In the centre of the political stage, the place of the weak left is taken by the strong right. Such is the logic of political struggle.

The left lacks the resolve to talk about bureaucracy. The far right talks about it. The left tries to show that international institutions are playing a beneficial role. The far right denies this. The masses listen, and quite soon come to understand that the propaganda of the left contains no less demagogy, at the very least, than that of the right.

The new realism came long ago to serve as a programme for the German Social Democrats, but this party has shown little capacity for winning power. Where the bourgeois parties are effective, there is no demand for the new realists. Only in 1998 did the situation change, mostly because of the internal crisis of the Conservative government.

Hence the new realism, the turn to 'moderation' and the search for 'consensus', which together made up the distinctive response of the left political establishment to the crisis of the movement, merely served to deepen this crisis. By the late 1990s the political structures of the left had discredited themselves to an unprecedented degree. Since the collapse of the Second International, the left had never been so demoralized and discredited. Meanwhile, as had happened repeatedly in the history of the left, the crisis of the movement had become most acute precisely during the period when the bankruptcy of capitalism as a world system was becoming most evident. Remaining mere spectators as the capitalist crisis unfolded, the members of the left were incapable either of replacing capitalism with a better society, or of reforming it, or even of helping it.

The newspaper, the *Independent*, characterized the views of British Labour leader Tony Blair as 'decent middle-class radicalism'.[69] Meanwhile the *Socialist Register* commented on New Labour's 'paralytic fear of seeming anti-capitalist'.[70] Earlier, the *Socialist Register* had criticized the party for opportunism and half-heartedness, finding in labourite socialism every possible fault from empiricism to primitive doctrinairism. All this, however, made sense only so long as the labourites had a certain notion of the need to change British society. The new leadership, while rejecting the party's traditional ideology, could not in practice suggest new goals. What was involved was not so much a sharp turn to the right as a complete loss of all reference points; it became impossible even to speak of strategic 'turns'.

It is instructive to observe that in no country of the world has an attempt to found a new party on the basis of new realist ideology been successful. The parties that have embraced this ideology have invariably been old organizations shamelessly exploiting their traditional social bases, which continue giving them support solely in memory of the services (revolutionary and reformist) these parties have rendered in the past. It is therefore no accident that in Eastern Europe the new realism has been represented by post-communists, and in the West by social democrats; both, for the workers of the countries concerned, have been the parties of the 'glorious past'.

The conservative-bureaucratic nature of the new realism is becoming more and more obvious despite copious outpourings of modernist rhetoric. What confronts us is not a new phase in the development of the left movement, but merely the shameful last stage in the degeneration of bureaucratic centralist organizations. They have long ago lost any notion of the reasons why they were once set up. The politics of the new realism constantly erodes the accustomed bond between the political apparatus and the masses, thus freeing up social energy for the emergence of new mass movements.

What About the Workers?

However great the loyalty of the traditional supporters of left parties might be, it has its limits. This is recognized by the politicians themselves. The moderate 'realists' wait in terror for a revolt by their own supporters. Meanwhile the radicals, seeing that this revolt cannot possibly happen, lose all respect for the proletariat.

While losing faith in the historic mission of the working class, the politicians have by no means ceased to believe in their own indispensability. But if the traditional idea of struggling for workers' liberation loses its hold, it becomes unclear for whom the party exists, and whom the parliamentary factions represent. One of the ideologues of the Spanish United Left, noting that the majority of workers preferred social democrats and even rightists, recommended that leftists orient to 'sectors of the youth and of the middle layers – that is to say, to groups of the population that at a particular moment can be motivated by ideology'.[71] In Russia, Aleksandr Buzgalin is certain that society 'is not simply divided into owners of capital and hired workers'. Of no less and perhaps even of more importance is 'the contradiction between conformists and those who are capable of joint social creativity'.[72] Traditional workers and trade union organizations, with their dull discipline and ideology of solidarity, thus appear hopelessly mired in the old world; independent intellectuals, by contrast, are the heralds of communism.

It is true that the discipline of a capitalist factory is a poor school of self-management and democracy. But non-conformism does not equal revolutionism either. In societies where innovations are becoming a requirement of the market, non-conformism may be no more than a manifestation of a sort of meta-conformism. Cooperatives and various experimental creative and productive associations give birth to their own norms and conventions which at times are no less rigid than the old industrial culture. The overwhelming majority of workers, doomed to struggle for their survival, simply cannot allow themselves the luxury of 'free creativity'. This possibility can arise before such people only spontaneously, in the process of social changes for which, in the view of the ideologues, they are quite unready.

Social democracy is also becoming more and more remote from the working class. Socialist parties, Sassoon notes, have come increasingly to be dominated by middle-class activists, and as a paradoxical result have come to reflect the class basis of post-industrial society more accurately.

> For instance, the typical member of the British Labour Party – one of the most class-bound parties of Europe, in terms of image and rhetoric – was, by 1989, middle-class, middle-aged and male. Only one in four members was a manual worker. Among the individual members of the Labour Party more belong to the white collar public sector union NALGO – not affiliated to the party – than any other union; more are members of the Association of University Teachers than of the National Union of Mineworkers.

In addition, the average Labour Party member is considerably richer than the average voter.[73] Among the representatives of the middle class, in turn, it is possible to observe a clear division between representatives of the public sector who gravitate to the left and the more right-wing employees of private enterprise. In this sense leftists in Britain, as in a number of other countries, have become representatives of institutions of the welfare state rather than of a particular class.

In most countries workers continue from inertia to vote for 'their' parties, but only because they have no alternative. The traditional industrial proletariat is increasingly losing touch with left politics, while the massive new layers of workers employed in science and in the service sector lack organic links with the left. With rare exceptions, the radical moods which arise in this milieu have no connection with either parliamentary or academic socialism.

'The question is not only of deciding what the strategy should be for introducing changes to programmes and developing new principles for parliamentary work and mobilizational tactics', wrote the Mexican political scientist Nayar Lopez Castellanos, 'but also of restoring the faith of the masses in the parties, of convincing the broad layers that are alarmed by the fall in their level of well-being (which is fully understandable) that active participation in political life is a real mechanism of social change'.[74]

By the late twentieth century the parliamentary practice of most left parties clearly contradicted this goal. 'What has been lethal for the left is the fact that its parties have been avenues for social climbing on the part of some of their members, and not organisms for change', wrote the Spanish commentator Enrique del Olmo:

> These practices and many others have created a left that is uncritical, apolitical, domesticated, deideologized, and lacking in political initiative both on the general and the day-to-day level. This is a left that passively contemplates the fact that it is in retreat, that it is pedalling without knowing where it is going, and that despite being aware of all this it is helpless to do anything about it.[75]

This is true not only of social democracy, but also to a significant degree of the radical left, including the extra-parliamentary and even the revolutionary left. These latter currents are the target of the ironic remark by the Spanish writer José Jimenez Lozano to the effect that there are obviously two sorts of 'reds' – 'the earlier type, who had ideals but nothing to eat', and the others, 'who were called "reds" for some other reason, but who could not really be reds'.[76] Membership in a strong left party opens certain prospects for personal success even if this party is in opposition. Left organizations serve as mechanisms providing vertical mobility for educated and active sons and daughters of the lower strata of society and for a section of the middle class. There is nothing intrinsically evil in this, especially since the left should not demand that its leaders and activists totally renounce the pleasures of life for the sake of rendering ascetic service to an idea. But these circumstances should be kept in mind. During the period of crisis of the political movement the activity of the left opposition is at risk of degenerating into another, more refined, variety of conformism.

The corrupting influence of parliamentary or academic institutions on radicals who enter their doors was already being noted in the nineteenth century. In earlier times, however, the left managed to develop a powerful antidote. This antidote was the link which parliamentarians and intellectuals possessed with the mass movement, and the profound ideologization of workers' parties. Whatever the drawbacks of the rigid ideology of traditional socialism, this ideology was infused with certain moral norms and requirements. Breaching these was impossible without severing one's links with the organization and, in turn, automatically losing any high position one held in the parliamentary system.

The de-ideologization of the labour movement was accompanied by an inevitable erosion of the moral demands made on leaders and intellectuals. As the centre of gravity shifted from the labour movement to the middle class, the traditional system of norms and values gradually disappeared. The left movement became ripe for the new morality in just the same way that the Christian Church by the early sixteenth century, had become ripe for the Reformation. The contempt for workers shown in intellectual left circles was matched only by the contempt for these circles shown by workers. And however numerous the new middle class in Western countries might have become, it proved incapable of developing its own morality. The natural rejection of an exclusive orientation toward industrial workers that took place as the world of labour underwent profound changes did not lead to the appearance of a new, broader ideology. Instead of trying to unite various groups of the exploited around itself, the left came to express the naive self-love of the 'broad' middle class. The only 'unification' that can be achieved on such a basis is between intellectuals and bureaucrats.

Returning to Struggle

Drawing up a balance sheet on the prolonged rule of the socialists in Spain, Jaime Pastor noted that the party elite used its presence in office in order to win as much autonomy as possible 'in relation to their own social base'. But the party's loss of power has not by any means prompted a moral cleansing. On the contrary, the period since the electoral defeat has seen 'a growing bipolarization between a "social-liberal" left preoccupied with coming to power at any price, and another with a weakness for sectarian abstention and for uncritically reaffirming its credentials from the past'.[77] This is not only true of Spain. The same can be said of the conflict between Tony Blair and supporters of Labour traditions in Britain, and of the endless discussions of the Communist Party of the Russian Federation and the Russian Communist Workers Party. Reiterating old slogans that have clearly lost their content does not permit one to break out of the vicious circle of concessions and defeats. The dogmatic left is doomed each time to support the 'realists' at the decisive movement in the struggle for power, since it is unable to develop its own alternative and has no chance of winning power itself. The socialist 'old believers' thus effectively become accomplices of the new realists, continually showing the impotence of their revolutionary thought and political practice. Actions are replaced by declarations, ideas by symbols and programmes by the reciting of principles. On the moral plane, the position of simple negation is just as dubious as that of reconciliation with reality. The result in both cases is the same: everything remains just as it was.

Everyone who goes to the market-place knows the first rule of trade: if you want a reasonable deal, ask for more than you expect to get. But leftist politicians, hypnotized by their own words about 'responsible management', have totally forgotten that their class enemy (excuse me, 'social partner') lives according to the laws of the market, and is incapable by nature of respecting any other laws. Leftists will not make any gains so long as the desire to reassure their adversaries proves stronger than their readiness to do anything for their own supporters.

Defeats are an inevitable part of politics. Not every struggle can be won, and by no means every risk should be taken. But, in any discussion, clarity is essential. The central question in the struggle for reforms is that of who secures concessions from whom. Only where the left forces are persistent and aggressive can they win a social compromise that is favourable for workers. Since the mid-1980s the thinking of the left has been dominated by a conscious or unconscious fear of defeat. This is not surprising after a train of setbacks. Pessimism has become the natural sequel to the triumphal illusions of previous decades. But must we be so fearful of defeats? Near the end of his life Jean-Paul Sartre said that the progress of humanity proceeds from failure to failure. It has happened more than once in history that battles that have ended in defeat have been decisive for securing victory in the war.

Setbacks in themselves are not so terrible. Far more dangerous is the inability of the left forces to respond correctly to these reverses.[78] In politics, knowing how to retreat means knowing how to sacrifice tactical positions for the sake of strategic goals, and understanding that it may be necessary to reject power in order to preserve the movement. Not least, it means remaining true to one's goals and principles in a period of setbacks. There is now a good deal of evidence to suggest that this period is nearing its end. Dissension and confusion are spreading in international financial centres. But if left-wing politicians, demoralized by their own misfortunes and lacking confidence in their strength, do not muster the resolve to present society with a serious programme of structural reforms, they will be routed in short order.

The new generation of leftists has to draw the unavoidable conclusions from the lessons of the 1980s. This new generation is taking shape today. Fearless of defeats, able to keep their feet on the ground in the case of victory, refusing to waste time on fruitless dogmatic wrangles, and equally ready for action on the streets, in the factories, in the parliamentary chambers or in the offices of state ministries, the members of this new generation will sooner or later make their presence felt.

2

De-Revising Marx

After the events of 1989–91 Marxian socialism, which 15 or 20 years earlier had seemed such a real force, again turned into a ghost. Constant attempts, involving all the efforts of professional exorcists, have since been made to finally lay Marx to rest. But the ghost has not departed.

Jacques Derrida in his controversial book *Specters of Marx* advised his readers to recall *The Communist Manifesto*, written in 1848.

> Today, almost a century and a half later, there are many who, throughout the world, seem just as convinced that what one is dealing with there is only a specter without body, without present reality, without actuality or effectivity, but this time it is supposed to be a past specter. It was only a specter, an illusion, a phantasm, or a ghost: that is what one hears everywhere today ('Horatio saies, 'tis but our Fantasie, /and will not let beleefe take hold of him'). A still worried sigh of relief: let us make sure that in the future it does not come back! At bottom, the specter is the future, it is always to come, it presents itself only as that which could come or come back; in the future, said powers of old Europe in the last century, it must not incarnate itself, either publicly or in secret. In the future, we hear everywhere today, it must not re-incarnate itself; it must not be allowed to come back since it is past.[1]

What is Revisionism?

The more life there is in Marx's views, the more natural the desire to bury him appears. No one strives to 'bury Hegel' or refute Voltaire, since it is clear even without this that Hegelianism and Voltairianism belong to the past. The ideas of the philosophers of the past have become dissolved in modern theories. With Marx this has not happened. Nor can it happen, since the society which he analysed, criticized and dreamed of changing is still alive. In this sense the end of Marxism can come only with the end of capitalism.

The tough, categorical conclusions of the great economist create discomfort; they make it difficult for people who seek compromise with the capitalist order to pursue moderate and flexible policies, and in the final analysis constitute a moral judgement on such individuals. It was because of this that the desire to revise Marxism arose almost simultaneously with the appearance of parliamentary workers' parties.

In order to become moderate, socialism had to pass through revisionism. If Marxism belongs to the past, then its harsh conclusions have lost their moral significance for contemporary society. All that remains of historical socialism is a set of general values, which everyone is free to interpret as he or she wishes. It is quite obvious that capitalism is changing, and it is therefore useless to wage war on it with the help of quotations from books written in the last century. Neither moderation nor compromise are sins in themselves. Under particular political conditions any serious party is doomed to have to seek compromises. In politics, one must not fail to take into account the relationship of forces.

But people ideologize their practice in their own peculiar fashion, and turn justifications of present-day actions into the ideology of the future. This means that a political conjuncture that is unfavourable for us is turned into an ideal state, a forced deviation into a wise strategy and weakness into valour. Where this has occurred, defeat becomes irreversible and tactical weakness becomes strategic impotence, while the goal of the movement, instead of being to transform society, becomes a more successful adaptation to it.

There is a flavour of commercial accounting about the very term 'revisionism'. We are not talking here about a rethinking or even a critique of Marxism, but about a mechanical calculation of the theoretical cash in hand, of the 'assets' and 'liabilities' of the doctrine. Following this accounting a few remaining values might be used, while the out-of-date ideological products are written off as scrap. In this rigidity and concreteness, revisionists are closely akin to the most hidebound among the orthodox. The only difference is that the latter cling to every item of the ideology, trying to prove, like some elderly householder, that it absolutely must be kept in the dwelling, just in case. Revisionist ideologues try to clear out the premises, discarding as quickly as possible everything that is 'superfluous'.

The analytical method of revisionism might best be called descriptive. Comparing the description of one or another social phenomenon in classical Marxism with modern reality, revisionists quite reasonably assert that there are differences. With this the study comes to an end, since the differences are seen as reasons in themselves for rejecting Marx's conclusions. There is no analysis here in the precise sense of the word; it is simply thought superfluous. The trouble is that reality continues to change. The events and processes described by the revisionists also vanish into the past, leaving their conclusions subject to doubt.

Historically, revisionist discourse was very important for the development of socialist thought. Bernstein's revisionism was the starting point for Lenin, Trotsky, Gramsci and so forth. The periodically recurring debates about the relevance of Marxism, and the latest revisions, mark the approach of a turning point in the history of the socialist movement and of socialist thought. These debates unquestionably bear witness to the crisis of Marxism or of its dominant interpretations, including revisionist ones.

Since official Soviet scholarship rejected its former orthodox approaches in the mid-1980s, a number of writers have tried to summarize the general conclusions of revisionism and to provide them with theoretical backing. Vladislav Inozemtsev writes that in the West during the twentieth century 'the internal bases of the social system have regenerated themselves in fundamental fashion, sometimes to an even greater degree where the whirlwinds of revolution and civil war have penetrated'. According to Inozemtsev, 'after the Great Depression and the Second World War Western society underwent changes which, although not particularly noticeable to the superficial observer, had by the mid-1960s placed this socium outside the boundaries of the capitalist system'. Western society was said to have entered a transitional phase, and all subsequent changes would take place 'in evolutionary fashion'.[2] In the course of this evolution all the goals of the former Marxist socialism were being achieved, but without upheavals, without class war, without expropriations or other unpleasantness, though not, of course, without social and political conflicts, the possibility of which not even the most moderate writer would deny.

This reference to the 1960s is very significant in a book that appeared in the 1990s. The work contains no analysis of neoliberalism or of the Eastern European reforms, although it would hardly seem that the author, living in Russia, could have failed to notice these phenomena. The problem here is not with forgetfulness but with methodology. Such argumentation is also characteristic of other writers. Recognizing the services rendered by Marx in the history of social thought, the editor-in-chief of the well-known academic journal *Polis*, I.K. Pantin, writes:

> The subsequent course of history has shown, however, that many of the problems of bourgeois society to which Marx pointed have begun to be resolved as capitalist production has developed (wage increases, the growth of mass consumption, social welfare legislation, the unification of capital and of the forces of government on a national and international level, intervention by the state in the economy, and so forth). More and more often it must be acknowledged that the canons of the Marxist critique of capitalism correspond more to the past than to the present, let alone the future.[3]

The genuine changes that took place in Western capitalism in the 1960s were perceived by the revisionist schools as the end of traditional capitalism. Eduard Bernstein viewed the changes occurring in Western society during his own time in similar fashion, though to his credit he refrained from drawing the simple conclusions embraced by later revisionist schools. Alas, while describing the 'new reality', none of the revisionists noticed how it was growing old. The Welfare State began everywhere to yield up its conquests. Market mechanisms began increasingly to free themselves from any form of regulation, state or international, while private property was affirmed as a sacred and universal principle.

Technological changes gave birth not to the economy of free creativity, but to the economy of cheap labour power. The intensity of exploitation began to increase. The dependency of workers on management began to grow, and wages fell not only in developing countries and the former communist states, but from the mid-1990s, in a number of Western countries as well.

It was, as German economist Winfried Wolf formulated, 'the return of normal capitalism'.[4]

Revisionist theoreticians have preferred to ignore neo-liberalism, or to present it as a temporary phenomenon which merely renders the generally harmonious development of society more complex. But neo-liberalism is not a 'zig-zag of development', nor an error of the politicians, but the trunk route of the evolution of capitalism. Its essence lies in the fact that bourgeois society can no longer allow itself to maintain the social achievements of previous decades. Although social democrats have correctly noted that the volume of resources that society allots for the solving of its social problems has increased significantly compared to the 1960s, this is irrevelant to the main point: that as capitalism becomes a global system, it is inevitably becoming both harsher and more profligate.

The Time of Reaction

The reaction that set in after 1989 differed from all previous reactions in that it succeeded in presenting itself in the guise of progress and modernization.

'In socialist jargon the terms "left-wing" and "progressive" have been virtually synonymous', writes the British historian Willie Thompson. The idea of progress has dominated modern consciousness, and the ideology and practice of the left has been perceived as the most consistent expression of this idea. As a result:

> the left, broadly defined, tended, except for the years of fascist ascendancy between 1933 and 1942, to be swimming with the cultural tide and making the political running; the right, however many successful actions it fought, seemed to be permanently on the defensive, or, after 1945, forced to adopt the stance that 'if you can't beat them, join them.' The belief that history is on one's side may be a consolatory myth, but it is significant that it was only to the left that this form of consolation was available, while the right had to make do with nostalgia.[5]

Everything changed radically from the mid-1980s. For the first time since the nineteenth century the bourgeoisie acquired an attacking ideology. Neo-liberalism succeeded in presenting itself as a force aiding modernization and dynamism, accusing the labour movement, the left and the trade unions of conservatism, of hostility to technical progress, and of a desire to sacrifice the future for the sake of immediate prosperity and 'privileges'. At the same time, confidence in progress itself had been shaken. The environmental, feminist and post-modernist criticism of the mainstream ideology was based not on a more radical concept of progress, but on a profound doubt in progress as such. This represented a natural and understandable rethinking of the historical experience of the nineteenth and twentieth centuries.[6] But for the left, this change of mood in society was catastrophic. 'With this shift in outlook the central cultural citadel of the left has fallen into the hands of its enemies and with consequences far more disabling than any of the specific routs that the left has suffered upon the political field.'[7]

As the theoreticians of the German Party of Democratic Socialism have noted, during the 1990s neo-liberal propaganda has managed to depict as obstacles to modernization and progress precisely those structures and relationships that had earlier been cited as proof of the 'civilized' nature of capitalism.[8] This is connected with the fact that the period of social reaction on the world scale has also been a time of technological renewal. This in itself is nothing new; something similar occurred in the first half of the nineteenth century, during the initial stages of the Industrial Revolution. Only later, and in hindsight, was it to become clear that new technologies do not strengthen the positions of triumphant reactionary elites, but undermine them. At the beginning of the century the introduction of new machines was accompanied directly by the defeat of bourgeois republicanism, by a dramatic weakening of the social position of hired workers, and by the installing of a 'new world order' within the framework of the Holy Alliance, the first precursor of the United Nations.

However paradoxical this might appear in hindsight, the first social consequence of the Industrial Revolution was a marked weakening of the position of the working class. The American economist Fred Block notes:

> In craft-based industries, such as Lyonese silk or Sheffield cutlery, workers were characteristically able to exercise a good

> deal of power at the workplace because of their possession of craft knowledge and their strong ties of collective solidarity. Moreover, the fact that they had craft knowledge made their position quite different from that of other workers. Although these craft workers sometimes had to endure bouts of unemployment brought about by the business cycle, they were much less likely to have to take whatever work happened to be offered. Their skill provided protection from market and employer coercion.[9]

On this basis, Block even concludes that it was not inevitable that the transition to a modern economy would be based on the mass production and unqualified labour typical of the second half of the nineteenth century, since there existed an 'alternative route based on specialized manufacturing and craft skills'.[10]

Marx also noted the exceptional social achievements of British workers on the eve of the Industrial Revolution, but in his view the desire of entrepreneurs to free themselves from the dictates of workers and to bind workers to new labour relations that were more advantageous for capital acted as one of the stimuli for the massive introduction of new machines during the Industrial Revolution. As a result of the Industrial Revolution, the European working class suffered a historic defeat.

It was only later, after the workers' movement had grown in strength thanks to the rise of modern trade unionism and the appearance of the first socialist parties, that reaction gave way to a new revolutionary upsurge. The experience of the century that followed has become fixed in a peculiar piece of labour movement mythology. Here I have in mind two extremely dangerous errors. In the first place, workers and their ideologues became convinced that any technological and industrial development strengthened their position. In the second place all these people, whether socialists or communists, reformists or revolutionaries, viewed history as a rectilinear process of constant movement toward more 'advanced' forms of social organization. The forces of reaction could, no doubt, retard or even halt this process, but they could not encroach upon the 'irreversible' gains of the workers.

The groundlessness of both these theses has been shown during the 1990s. In this sense, the defeats suffered by the forces of the left during this period have been far more serious and demoralizing than all the previous blows of the twentieth century. It has been revealed that history does not move in a straight line. The collapse of the historical illusions of the left and the labour movement has been accompanied by an unprecedented crisis of values and loss of self-confidence, although the only strategies that were really defeated were the rectilinear ones based on a mechanistic vision of social progress.

It is significant that the revisionists of the 1980s and 1990s underestimated the significance and scale of the neo-liberal reaction in just the same way as orthodox Marxists in the 1960s were unwilling to see the changes occurring then. The events of the 1990s have shown that if the underlying nature of capitalism has changed at all, these changes have been substantially less than moderate-left theoreticians would have wished. Meanwhile, the 'new phenomena' to which these theoreticians referred were to a considerable degree the result of class struggle and of the conflict of the two systems – in other words, they were forced on capitalism from outside.

Escaping from Utopia

After the 'end of history', history in complete accord with Fukuyama's ideas is beginning again. The question inevitably presents itself: who is old-fashioned now? Since the demise of the welfare state the world has not become either more stable or more just, or even more free, since the turning of violence into a norm of social life is devaluing civil liberties. But while exposing the vices of the new world order, leftists are not countering it with their own ideology.

> The left has to accept the fact that the Marxist project for revolution launched by the *Communist Manifesto* is dead. There will certainly be revolutions ... but they will not be explicitly socialist ones that follow the Marxist tradition begun by the First International.[11]

The American Roger Burbach and the Nicaraguan Orlando Nunez see the only alternative to neo-liberalism in spontaneous movements that express basic needs. A new, more just society 'will have to come out of an amalgam of the different national, ethnic and cultural movements of the world'.[12]

Despite the fact that many such movements are openly reactionary, leftists are not finding in themselves the strength to condemn them, since the left itself has lost its psychological and moral footing. Without the traditional principles of socialism, the left no longer has clear criteria for judging what is progressive and what is reactionary, or even any serious idea of the role which 'national, ethnic and cultural' movements play within the system of world order/disorder. Even the fact that most such movements in Eastern Europe have embraced neo-liberal economic programmes does not embarrass today's Western leftists. In the eyes of these people, manifestations of a new barbarism are becoming indistinguishable from the struggle for the rights of workers.

> Today people are willing to fight and die for their ethnic and national identities. However, unlike the early and mid-twentieth century, few will fight for socialism. Only when new movements for social justice and postmodern socialisms have sunk deep roots around the globe and become wedded to people's most basic needs and interests will we have a powerful banner that mobilizes individuals to dramatically change the world they live on.[13]

Until such ideas somehow take root it is evidently up to us either to endure the outrages of neo-liberalism, or to support any and all ethnic movements, including those whose leaders take the first chance to establish contacts with the International Monetary Fund, the World Bank or the King of Saudi Arabia.

The masses who made the Russian revolutions of 1905 and 1917 were not inspired by Marxist ideas either. People followed the Bolsheviks not because Lenin and Trotsky had a more developed theory of socialism, but because the Bolsheviks put forward the slogans of peace, land and social justice. What works is not ideology but a concrete programme. It would have been a different matter if the Bolsheviks had not managed in good time to formulate their slogans that expressed the interests of the masses – if they had not been Marxists, and had not had an exceptional grasp of the dynamic of the revolutionary process and of the class struggle.

So long as the struggle against oppression is not at the same time a struggle for a new society, it is doomed to defeat. Indeed, the reality is even worse; the discrediting of progressive utopianism in mass consciousness can have only one, inevitable result: its place will be taken by a reactionary utopia.

Unless there is a clear idea of the goal, it is impossible to work out either strategy or tactics. Lenin considered that the main service rendered by social democracy at the end of the nineteenth and the beginning of the twentieth centuries was to unite Marxism with the workers' movement. This explosive mixture really did shake the world. Lenin, as a genuine follower of the traditions of Enlightenment, was convinced that proletarian consciousness would readily penetrate the masses with the help of the intelligentsia. In reality the process was mutual. The masses could not elaborate theory, but without links to the mass movement theory becomes ossified. When Marx's ideas became the ideology of the workers' movement they underwent a transformation, and became Marxism.

It is entirely natural that a theoretician is obliged to be more radical than a practical activist. Still, Marx made a distinction between compromises in politics and in thought. If compromise is allowable for a politician, a thinker has to maintain a 'simple moral tact' where it is concerned.[14] That which is possible is not always obligatory. Politics is the art of compromise, and here the possibility of a divorce between theory and practice is already present. The concrete actions of Lenin, Trotsky or Gramsci did not necessarily flow from their theoretical constructs (this is illustrated in compelling fashion by the contrast between their writings in periods of action and the texts they composed during periods in prison or emigration). But the practical activity of the representatives of classical Marxism nevertheless remained closely linked to their theoretical quests. In the post-war period this link was severed.

Marxism has indeed suffered a historic defeat. However, this did not come at the end of the 1980s when the Berlin Wall fell, but much earlier, when theory again became detached and isolated from the movement. This did not happen only in the East with the founding of Stalinist 'Marxism-Leninism'. As early as the 1930s Marxism in the West became the province of academic circles, while for social democracy and the communist parties the general 'classical' formulae remained no more than dead letters.

In the 1990s the rituals were discarded. This was easy because it had been a long time since anyone had given any thought to their meaning. We returned to the starting point, when theory and the mass movement were quite disconnected. But the two are not separated by an insurmountable wall. The fact that a significant layer of workers has only a very dim notion of socialist ideas does not mean that these ideas should not be propagated.

Intellectuals who have lost their political reference points do not need much to satisfy them: 'Any policy can be called socialist if it is aimed at limiting the elemental character of the market and at redistributing incomes.'[15] However, redistribution does not always serve the ends of social justice, and the basic needs of most people will not be guaranteed without structural reforms. Here is the paradox, in the fact that 'simple' demands – for schools, hospitals, roads – turn out to be the most difficult to meet. So long as the neo-liberal order remains in place, there will never be enough money for them.

The socialist project has to be translated into a language that people understand. This is not the language, cultivated by Western intellectuals, of postmodernist radicalism and multiculturalism. It is the simple, blunt language of classical Marxism.

Marx began by trying to cleanse the socialist project of utopianism. He did not succeed completely, for the simple reason that there is invariably a utopian dimension in any social idea and in any project. However, Marx's decisive contribution to political theory lay in the fact that he showed the necessity and possibility of abandoning utopian day-dreaming in favour of seeking practical change. Rejecting pragmatism, the Marxist tradition proclaimed the need to unite idealism (in terms of fidelity to aims and principles) with the political realism of concrete actions. It is the experience of practical change that transforms socialist thought into science. Except within a context of political practice, therefore, such theory simply has no point.

Often through no fault of its own, Western academic Marxism is alienated from the mass movement and political action, and despite its enormous intellectual successes has gradually lost the ability to distinguish between theory and utopia. At the same time, the neo-liberal counter-offensive against socialism has gone ahead beneath the banner of 'anti-utopianism'. It is significant, however, that by the 1990s leftists themselves had become completely reconciled to the charge of 'utopianism'. Some, declaring themselves 'realists', had sworn to purge themselves of this utopianism (and of basic honesty along with it). Others, holding true to their ideals, began cultivating the utopian tradition within socialism. Evidence of this can be found in the very names of left journals – *Utope-kreativ* in Germany, *Utopias* in Spain, *Utopie-critique* in France and so forth. Supporters of the anti-capitalist left try to prove the need for a 'concrete utopia'.[16]

In effect, the left is facing the same need that confronted it a hundred years ago: to take the step from utopia to theory, from dreams to reality. This does not mean that utopian traditions should be condemned or banished, but they have to be overcome in the dialectical, Marxist sense. Without renouncing utopias, we have to step resolutely outside their bounds. In this sense we have to regenerate the again indispensable anti-utopian zeal of Marxian socialism.

Reclaiming the Tradition

The weakness of the left was a real fact of political life in the 1990s. Anti-capitalist politics must therefore take on a defensive character. Resistance to the offensive of capital is the message of the moment. But this resistance has to be strong and effective. It has to be based on a clear and sober understanding of the situation, of the left's own capacities and of the goals of the adversary. Ideological concessions weaken one's resistance. In politics, clear goals and confidence in the justice of one's cause are indispensable conditions for victory. Concessions do not open up new possibilities for making advances. The paradox of the late twentieth century lies in the fact that the very weakness of the left obliges it to be uncompromising. With the present relationship of forces, there can be no 'new consensus' or 'conditions, favourable to workers, for a new social compromise'. Everyone who dreams of reforms must first struggle to change the relationship of forces, and this means becoming a revolutionary and a radical in the traditional sense.

All consciousness is limited. There cannot be complete knowledge. A return from ill-defined and ambiguous post-Marxist theorizing to the tough, simple truths of classical Marxism is an essential condition of effective political practice, even if we now have an exquisite understanding of the restricted nature (but not falsehood) of many of Marx's original premises.

De-revising Marxism does not mean being dogmatic. The revolutionary socialism of the early years after 1917 was innovative but anti-revisionist. A call to embrace traditional values has nothing in common with rejecting dialogue or leading a hermetic existence. The active affirmation of tradition requires interaction with the outside world.

From the time of the Reformation, neo-traditionalism has been the ideology of revolutionaries. Martin Luther, calling for a return to the Bible, was a typical neo-traditionalist. Under the slogan of restoring traditional piety, the English puritans carried out an immense social overturn, opening up a new era in the history of their own country and of Europe. This traditionalism had nothing in common with conservatism. In the name of traditional values and principles, the world that had perverted and rejected these principles was repudiated. The result was change and innovation.

A return to traditions is among the most effective of mobilizing methods. Tradition is what is familiar, understandable and accessible to the masses. At the same time, it stands opposed to the soulless pragmatism and egoism of the elites. Except in relation to traditions, new ideas are not assimilated by popular consciousness. Revolts against injustice always rest on traditional ideas of justice. The fact that, in the process of struggle, tradition itself may undergo radical changes is something quite different. Islamic fundamentalism is a very efficient modern reaction to capitalist westernization. A profoundly reactionary form of protest, fundamentalism has enjoyed unprecedented success for the reason that, while incorporating the experience of the twentieth century, it has returned to the masses a confidence in their own culture.

Western sociologists, recognizing fundamentalism as a new phenomenon (Anthony Giddens notes that until 1950 the word did not even exist in the English language), experience obvious discomfort when they encounter it. Giddens repeats constantly that fundamentalism 'is nothing other than tradition defined in the traditional way – but in response to novel circumstances of global communications'.[17] This, however, is the whole point – that under new conditions tradition cannot be defended by traditional methods. In the age of Muhammad there were neither plastic bombs nor terrorist suicides. The Internet with its Islamic sites did not exist, and neither did the forms of mobilization characteristic of the new mass movements.

Fundamentalism has little in common with traditional Islam, which suffered defeat in its collision with the West. That Islam continues to exist in parallel with fundamentalism, and is gradually giving way to it. In societies which have not been radically modernized, there is no fundamentalism. Only where tradition has been undermined or destroyed has fundamentalism been able, as it were, to construct it afresh, in a shape appropriate to the realities and opportunities of the late twentieth and early twenty-first centuries.

Islamic fundamentalism, despite the ideas of Giddens and of liberal journalists, is quite unlike a closed system that rejects everything 'alien'. On the contrary, it continually assimilates new methods and new experience. It is open to the world, but open in an aggressive manner, on the offensive. Here lies its real danger, just like the danger of the new European nationalism, which cannot be explained using simple references to traditions of populism and fascism surviving in this or that country since the 1930s. Offensive action sharply changes the meaning of tradition, which is no longer simply preserved but affirmed. It is renewed, and enriched with new experience.

Those who appeal to tradition include not only the insurgent poor, but also elites striving to regain lost positions. Neo-liberalism is one of the most significant examples of neo-traditionalist ideology. Needing to counter socialism with their own offensive project, the ideologues of the financial bourgeoisie did not start inventing new ideas. On the contrary, they turned to their traditional, classical programme, finding inspiration in the works of the theoreticians of the golden age of liberal capitalism. Meanwhile, neo-liberalism and the neo-classical school in economics are nothing like a mechanical recycling of the old liberalism. Even Adam Smith's 'invisible hand', to which continual references are made, was by no means the British economist's central idea.

At the same time as the reactionary forces are making active use of tradition, the left has proven incapable of doing this, since it has lost its main tradition, of active struggle against capitalism. If socialists want to become a real force again, they must also return to their basic propositions. This is gradually beginning to be recognized by theoreticians, although the politicians still reject it. Oskar Negt, who is probably the last theoretician of the Frankfurt School, writes that on the threshold of the new century the left needs to 'return to its tradition'.[18] The same view is held by André Brie, one of the ideologues of the Party of Democratic Socialism in Germany. Appealing for a radical renewal of the visions and perspectives of the left, he stresses: 'Modern socialist thought for me is also a – critical – return to Marx (and at the same time a turn to addressing new questions of contemporary capitalist society and to taking up global challenges).'[19]

It is precisely tradition that allows the creation of new organizations. In Turkey in 1996 socialist groups, after overcoming a long period of sectarianism, managed to unite in a single party. Ufik Uras, the 36-year-old who was elected as its leader, declared: 'I define myself as a Marxist, with a concept of Marxism that is based on a return to first principles.'[20]

What is involved here is not a refined nostalgia for some golden age of the labour movement, although using nostalgia for political propaganda is perfectly acceptable and very effective. The point is simply that where the left decides to be true to itself, it succeeds in regaining the political initiative. Society experiences the need for new ideas and strong traditions in equal degree. Neo-liberalism can no longer furnish either the one or the other. The left can provide them, but lacks the will to do so.

A return to Marxism means above all restoring the centrality of class in the political thinking of the left. Classical Marxism never argued that the contradiction between labour and capital was the only contradiction present in society, or necessarily the most acute. Nor did Marx and Engels assert that society was divided totally and without exception into classes (it is enough to recall their argument that in Germany in the early nineteenth century there were no classes). Marx and Engels merely asserted (and quite rightly) that the contradiction between labour and capital was crucial, and that without it other problems and contradictions could not be resolved. Class reductionism has in fact been a real characteristic of the Marxist tradition. Having understood the 'central' contradiction of the epoch, many Marxist have, as it were, liberated themselves from the need to think about the 'secondary' ones. Meanwhile, a secondary contradiction is no less real than the main one, and understanding the one without the other is impossible. This is why Marxist analysis has been beset by a growing poverty, vapidity, schematism and primitivism; in the final analysis, these have served to discredit the entire Marxist tradition.

While conscious of the richness and variety of social life, we must not forget that it is structured in a particular way. Many sociologists in the West note that class no longer plays the same pervasive role as before in society and in people's lives, especially since people define their social status more through consumption than production. In Eastern Europe and Latin America we see a widespread de-classing of workers and an atomization of the masses.[21] Nevertheless, consumption is impossible without production, and de-classing is impossible without class structures. The contradiction between labour and capital remains central and fundamental despite the appearance of a multitude of new problems and the exacerbation of old ones.

The conflict between labour and capital is not only a clash of interests, but also involves a counterposing of values, principles and morals. Only an ethical socialism that rests on a firm basis can have a positive meaning. We need to have a firm knowledge of which side we are on.

In 1996 the hit of the Russian musical season was a disk entitled 'Old Songs about the Most Important Thing'. This was a remake of old Soviet-era songs performed by post-Soviet stars. The buyers of this recording were not nostalgic veterans of the Stalin era – such people preferred the original versions. The huge success of the disk was due to its popularity among young people who could scarcely recall life in the Soviet Union. The new performances allowed them to experience songs about the most important thing – that which they could not hear about in postmodernist songs. About that which really was the most important thing.

The public demand for a sort of remake of historical Marxism makes itself felt at every step. It is this which represents the main basic need of present-day humanity; meeting it is the main, and in essence, the sole task of the modern left movement. If we do not cope with this task, our lives will have neither meaning nor justification.

3

The Return of the Proletariat

Rapid cutbacks in the number of jobs in the industrially developed capitalist countries have provided the starting point for sociological theories about 'the end of the proletariat', and even about 'the end of work'. The American sociologist Jeremy Rifkind declared confidently in the mid-1990s that we were on the 'road to a near-workless economy'.[1] Whole decades earlier, the French Marxist André Gorz had announced the end of the proletariat.[2]

Among leftists, an enthusiastic interest in new social perspectives linked to changed technologies had been superimposed on disillusionment with the historic mission of the working class. It was wrong, Oskar Negt wrote in 1996, to say that Marx had underestimated the vitality of capitalism; he had merely 'overestimated the capacity of the working class to do away with capitalism before the system took on barbaric forms'.[3] Two of the ideologues of the German Party of Democratic Socialism, the brothers André and Michael Brie, were even more bitter: 'Even for the entrepreneurs and their political representatives it is very difficult to formulate and project common positions, to be a "class for itself". The working class has appeared as a class for itself practically nowhere on earth in the last decades.'[4]

Post-industrial Mirage

Scepticism concerning the potential of the working class has been a perfectly natural result of the series of defeats suffered during the 1980s and 1990s. These were defeats not only for specific participants, for parties and trade unions, but also for the traditional class politics of the left. It was perhaps for this reason that a rapt anticipation of post-industrial society was especially typical of moderately left writers during the mid-1990s in Russia, where no signs of rapid technological advance were evident, but where the labour movement had displayed complete political impotence.

Over a period of about ten years supporters and opponents of the 'end of the proletariat' thesis repeated the same arguments and counter-arguments, while the discussion made no headway. Meanwhile the 1990s, despite massive technological changes (and in part, thanks to them), have not only failed to bring us any closer to post-industrial society, but on the contrary have demonstrated the totally abstract nature of this theory. It is significant that most of the supporters of the concept, while referring constantly to new global processes, make use almost exclusively of materials dealing with Western Europe and the United States. Taking issue with Rifkind, the New York *Left Business Observer* recalled as follows:

> People have been worrying about machines replacing human labor since the beginning of capitalism. Yes, machines do replace workers – but employment nonetheless continues to expand, quadrupling in the US over the last sixty years. In most parts of the world, aside from Europe and Africa, employment is growing. Throughout history, capitalism has constantly drawn new people into paid labor, though the demand for jobs always outstrips the system's capacity to provide them.[5]

Technology does not exist on its own; it can develop only within society. Technological breakthroughs have always been essential to the capitalist system as a means of placing pressure on workers. Abrupt rises in the technological level of production have almost always led to the devaluation of labour power and to increased unemployment. But this in turn has made human labour more profitable for entrepreneurs, and has therefore sharply reduced the stimulus to further technological innovations; at a certain point even very sophisticated machines start becoming uncompetitive with very cheap workers.

The French researcher Domenique Schapper notes that reductions in labour time and changes in the nature of work do not in themselves constitute evidence of changes in the central, system-defining role of labour in society. The mere citing of statistical data does not show that a process has been understood, especially when attempts are made to extrapolate trends mechanically into the future. The end of work is an idea of bureaucrats.[6]

Fashionable sociological theories aside, traditional industry and the working class are not disappearing from the modern world.[7] What is happening is that the world division of labour is undergoing dramatic changes. Traditional industrial production is more and more being transferred from the countries of the capitalist centre to those of the periphery and semi-periphery.

Even in the West, the traditional worker remains a typical figure. The French sociologists Gilles Balbastre and Joelle Stechel note a striking gap between the reality and the popular perceptions of it. Television programmes portray a France 'from which industrial production seems to have vanished'.[8] Meanwhile, 27 per cent of the economically active population are industrial workers, who reminded society of their existence during the massive strikes of 1995. The British sociologist Anthony Giddens points out that the division between the sphere of production and the sphere of services is becoming merely relative.

> A high proportion of the growth in service employment is due to the contribution those in such employment make to the production of goods in final consumption. it is, in other words, in large part an expression of the complexity of the division of labour. The coordination of modern industry, geographically dispersed and incorporated in an international division of labour, involves a high proportion of employees distant from the direct manufacture of goods but nevertheless integral to their production and consumption.[9]

According to the *New York Times*, between 1979 and 1995 more than 43 million jobs were eliminated in the US. Significant cuts in employment made their effects felt on skilled, well-educated and highly paid workers.

> Yet this is not a saga about rampant unemployment, as in the Great Depression, but one about an emerging redefinition of employment. There has been an increase of 27 million jobs in America since 1979, enough to easily absorb all the laid-off workers plus the new people beginning careers, and the national unemployment rate is low.[10]

A situation is arising in which workers are more and more often being laid off, against the background of an overall decline in unemployment. The total number of non-farm jobs in the US grew from 90 million in 1979 to 117 million in 1995.

Statistics show that the causes of present-day unemployment are not purely technological, but also social and economic. The mass sackings of workers cannot be put down to a rapid growth in the productivity of labour stemming from the new technologies. 'During the 1970s and 1980s US productivity grew at less than half its pace in the 1950s', Simon Head notes in a survey of the state of the American economy in the mid-1990s.

> Nevertheless, between 1973 and 1995 output per person of all non-farm workers in the private sector still rose by 25 percent, while the real hourly earnings of production and non-supervisory workers fell by 12 percent. During the present recovery, increases in real wages have not matched increases in productivity. Between 1990 and 1995 the productivity of all non-farm private sector employees increased by 10.3 per cent, while during the same period the real hourly wages of rank and file workers were unchanged. This is the first time in American postwar history that the real wages of most workers have failed to increase during a recovery.[11]

At the same time, job insecurity has increased. In complete accordance with classical Marxist theory, the growth of the reserve army of labour is placing extra pressure on workers, and lowering the cost of labour power. 'The sting is in the nature of the replacement work', the *New York Times* admits:

> Whereas 25 years ago the vast majority of the people who were laid off found jobs that paid as well as their old ones, Labor Department numbers show that now only about 35 per cent of laid-off fulltime workers end up in equally remunerative or better paid jobs.[12]

In sum, average wages after inflation fell between 1979 and 1995 by 3 per cent.

International statistics do not bear out the 'end of work' thesis either. Nor do they confirm the theories of fashionable futurologists in the late 1980s to the effect that self-employment, part-time work and other forms of 'free' labour activity are likely to take the place of hired labour. According to the International Labour Organization, 'while there has been some increase in self-employment, this has not meant the disappearance of regular jobs'.[13] Higher levels of unemployment are to be observed not in the countries that have taken the lead in technological development, but on the contrary, in the countries whose economies are growing slowly or are in crisis. As a rule, these are countries that are backward in technological terms. As for part-time work, statistics show that many workers choose it voluntarily 'for non-economic reasons'. How often this choice is really voluntary is the subject of debate (often, the workers involved are women who are forced to divide their time between family and work), but technology is not a factor here. Meanwhile, as *Left Business Observer* remarks, 'overwork is at least as characteristic of the labour market as is underwork'.[14]

It is not technology that determines how the economy evolves; on the contrary, the needs of the economy dictate that new technological methods must be implanted. Naturally, technological changes in their turn cannot fail to require a new organization of labour. But here as well, the changes have a significance quite different from what the theoreticians of 'post-industrial society' suppose. The organization of labour depends not only on technology, but also on the relationship of forces between labour and capital in the enterprise. The efforts by large corporations to avoid having workers concentrated in large plants is quite understandable. Modern methods of organizing production, such as lean production, re-engineering and outsourcing, are not aimed at forcing out traditional workers but at controlling them and forcing them to work more intensively.

All this is evidence not of the disappearance of the working class, but of the restructuring of the system of hired labour and of the simultaneous intensification of its exploitation. The threat of unemployment also forces people to work more for the same money.[15] The *New York Times* notes that in enterprises where significant job cuts have taken place, employees 'work more hours, take fewer vacation days or accept lesser benefits to keep their jobs'.[16] These, in general, are the same phenomena that Marx described in relation to the emergence under capitalism of the 'reserve army of labour'. As the *New York Times* acknowledges, technological changes are far from accounting for all job losses. The decisive factor is the economic system itself.

The members of the corporate elite hope that the constant threat of unemployment will raise workers' productivity. Meanwhile, the *New York Times* admits that workers often react by becoming less loyal to the firm. Wage cuts and the threat of unemployment also arouse a new wave of politicization.

> The floating anger is also influencing people's attitude toward politics. Pollsters say it is making centrist politics harder to practise and making people less faithful to any one party, less likely to vote and more willing to entertain the idea of a third party.[17]

But since 1989 demoralized leftists have been moving to the centre, and the role of mouthpieces for popular anger has been taken over by right-wing populists.

Technological Aristocracy

Noting the growth in the exploitation of traditional workers, whether blue collar or white collar, economists have turned their attention to the fact that within the framework of large corporations a new layer of 'technological aristocracy' is arising; in part, these people occupy the same place as the 'worker aristocracy' of the early twentieth century. In the new technological reality, the important thing is not so much knowledge of a machine as a worker's individual talents. As Fred Block observes, the modernization of production and the spread of robotization are creating an 'increasing need for employees with broad conceptual skills'. In fields where the use of industrial robots is becoming widespread, every second new job 'will require two or more years of college education'.[18] This is a little like the situation that applies in pre-industrial handicraft production: the tools are everywhere similar, but the process of production and the end product may be quite different, depending not only on the techniques used but also on the approach taken by the worker. However paradoxical it might seem, this could again strengthen the position of workers in relation to entrepreneurs. The more the process of labour becomes individualized, the more difficult it is to find replacements for the workers involved. Economists note that the new technologies and the accompanying forms of organization of labour are making management more difficult.

> Companies now rely more on networks of consultants, business service providers and suppliers; vertical integration is no longer regarded as, in itself, the best option for the coordination of economic activity. As companies have moved in this direction, however, they have had to learn to coordinate the activities of growing numbers of often physically distant providers over whom they lack direct, bureaucratic control.[19]

This also limits the opportunities for super-exploitation. Simon Head argues:

> The skills of the technical aristocracy who design software and reengineer work forces will remain in strong demand among corporations that cannot afford to lag behind in the competition in technological innovation. But since such skills are difficult to acquire, they will remain in short supply, and their price will continue to rise.[20]

Such processes are also to be observed in the 'newly industrializing countries'. Korean economists have begun to speak of a 'new generation' of workers, who are playing an ever-increasing role in corporations.

> The kind of employee sought by companies changes with the times. In the past, when companies were in the development stage, those who would work blindly for the interests of the organization were the most sought after. Now those companies that have entered an advanced phase need creative and progressive specialists who can better synthesize operations. The dawn of Korea's information age simply cannot be ignored. As more of the new generation enters the workforce, companies must cultivate the know-how for better managing their new structures ... The problem is, do Korean companies have such a capability?[21]

Mainstream economists see this problem as purely organizational. However, it poses a serious challenge to the very system of capitalist managment. Effective use of workers' potential becomes impossible unless there is a serious redistribution of power in the enterprise. Block compares the new situation with the one that existed in pre-industrial craft enterprises.

> The contemporary equivalent of craft knowledge is professional knowledge, and there are many examples of private firms that are quite sucessful despite the fact that most of their employees are professionals who are well insulated from the normal forms of coercion.[22]

The paradox lies in the fact that the workers themselves and their organizations still have not realized all the advantages that have arisen as a result of this situation, and have not been able to unite themselves in order to exploit these advantages to the fullest.

In describing the perspectives of the new technological elite, the Russian political scientist Aleksandr Tarasov argues that Marx was too hasty in identifying the anti-capitalist revolution with industrial workers, since 'the revolutionary subject has to appear, as might now be said, outside the System'.[23] Industrial workers cannot break through the limitations of the logic of the capitalist factory. It was not peasants who destroyed feudalism but the bourgeoisie, which, despite being hemmed in by the feudal estate, was not directly exploited by it. In precisely the same fashion, the anti-capitalist revolution will be consummated when the new technological elite to which the bourgeoisie has given birth sets out to get rid of it.

Post-industrial workers are to be found outside the system and at the same time within it. On the one hand:

> a mode of production that is founded on knowledge turns out to be one ... under which it is possible to overcome alienation. Knowledge is inalienable from its creator and bearer. This person controls the whole process of the 'production' of knowledge.

On the other hand, capitalism must continually attempt to transform the mass of producers of knowledge into 'a class of hired intellectual workers'.[24] The owners of capital try to establish control over the creative process, and this inevitably provokes opposition. The use of traditional capitalist methods of control over workers within the firm is rendered more difficult by the fact that the computer breaks down the boundary between work and leisure, free time and work time, since it is at the same time a means both of production and of leisure. Some 'serious' programmes include game-like elements, and vice versa.

The computer technologies specialist Yury Zatuliveter comes to a similar conclusion, arguing that the tasks of technological development impel the people carrying them out to take radical positions. 'The main task associated with computers', he maintains, does not consist in devising more perfect programmes, but in transforming society.[25] So far during the 1990s, the technological elite has not displayed any particular revolutionary potential. In no way does it perceive itself as an independent social and political force. Instead, it tries to use its advantages to improve its bargaining position. But it does not follow that things will always be thus. The Western bourgeoisie did not immediately become a revolutionary counter-elite either. In its early period it coexisted amicably with feudal hierarchs, and supported the strengthening of the absolutist state with which it was later to enter into conflict.

Whether a social layer is capable of carrying out social transformations depends not only on its status in society, but also on its ideology and level of political and social organization. The weak consciousness of the new layers of workers stems to a considerable degree from the inadequacies of the work that leftists have carried out with them. Of course, class consciousness is not imparted to workers from outside, as Lenin argued in *What is to be Done?* But neither does it arise in purely spontaneous fashion. Innovative ideology is the result of a historical encounter between the radical intelligentsia and a mass social layer that feels the need for new ideas. In this case, no such encounter has yet occurred.

As the new economic sectors develop, the position of the technological aristocracy that is concentrated in them becomes more and more vulnerable. The technological revolution of the late twentieth century is developing according to the same logic as the Industrial Revolution of the eighteenth and nineteenth centuries. This is the case not only with the production of computers and other modern equipment, but also with the intellectual products themselves. The demands by software firms for increases in the productivity of labour set in train the same processes already witnessed in the traditional sectors. Zatuliveter notes:

> Unlike industrial forms of the design and production of equipment, the production of programmes has remained in the phase of artisan labour, with the predominance of the human factor making the volume of production directly dependent on the number of adequately qualified people who can be attracted. It is not hard to see that thanks to massive computerization almost the entire intellectual resource has already been activated. Virtually everyone who is capable of programming computers is already programming them. This exacerbates to an extreme degree the problems involved in increasing the output of programmes with the help of programming technologies oriented toward the human factor. The resolving of this problem will lead to the collapse of artisan (extensive) forms of software production, and will result in a shift to industrial (intensive) forms, with the volumes of production expanding mainly through increases in the productivity of labour.[26]

A concentration of production is taking place, with the effect of bringing more and more programmers together in the staff of particular firms. Within the milieu of the programmers, the need for self-organization is increasingly coming to be felt, along with an understanding by these workers of their subordinate and dependent position. The exploitation of their labour is becoming intensified as well. Resistance to the supremacy of capital is growing. All this is strikingly similar to the processes described by Marx and his pupils with reference to industrial capitalism.

As the breadth of application of the new technologies increases and the number of specialists able to use them grows, the pressure on the workers in the modern sector increases as well. The logic of capitalism demands that the traditional factory discipline be extended to include them. However, replacing one specialist with another remains a relatively difficult matter, since the work itself is becoming more and more individual in quality, and training workers needs time. The result, as Block notes, is that 'managerial coercion tends to be weakened because of the need to maintain continuity of production'. Moreover, 'supervision itself can become problematic at high levels of skill; management acting unilaterally might simply not be able to figure out the most efficient way to organize the labor force and the distribution of tasks'.[27] Workers of the new type are more capable of resistance, including on an individual basis, and also of self-management. The greater the pressure on such workers, the more rapidly they become conscious of their role in society, and of the contradictions between their own interests and the logic of development of capital.

The Crocodile Phenomenon

The first wave of the technological revolution struck at blue-collar workers. In the mid-1980s all writers on the topic were united in observing a sharp decline in the share represented by industry in the overall structure of employment. By the end of the 1980s no more than 17 per cent of the US workforce remained in industry, significantly fewer than in the area of services. Analogous tendencies were observed in other developed countries, with the possible exception of Japan.[28]

This process has also affected the developing countries. A collective study devoted to workers in Third World countries notes that even in the most industrialized societies, proletarianization is going ahead in forms quite different from those in Europe, and on a quite different scale:

> Because of the higher productivity of modern industrial technology, the spread of wage-earning underway will never lead to a nucleus of industrial wage labour as great as that in Europe and the United States, where as much as 50 per cent of the labour force was at one point employed in industry. The level will probably never be attained in the industrializing third world, and this has led to the suggestion that the industrial working class will not have such a unifying and dominant role in the whole labour movement as was the case in early industrialized countries.[29]

The fact that in Japan, the technological leader of the capitalist world during the 1980s and most of the 1990s, the decline of industrial employment has been less and has proceeded much more slowly than in other countries testifies to the fact that it is too early to speak of the 'end of the proletariat'. During the period of unquestioned US hegemony in the world economy, industrial workers made up a substantially higher proportion of the workforce in the US than in Japan, but by the mid-1990s the proportion of Japanese workers employed in industry was substantially greater than the proportion in America. The rapid economic ascent of South Korea has also been accompanied by growth in the numbers of the industrial proletariat and in its weight within society. In April 1996 the *Korea Times* published a detailed survey of the state of the national economy. As the newspaper remarked, 'Manufacturing led the growth with a rapid increase in facility investment in the heavy and chemical sector.' Rapid growth was observed in shipbuilding, electronics and vehicle manufacturing. This also stimulated metallurgy, which according to experts had begun by the mid-1990s to 'reverse its earlier decrease rate to an increase'. Despite lower prices, output in the textile industry was continuing to grow as well. The growth of wages in Korea had led to an expansion of 'knock-down assembly sites in Asia and Eastern Europe'.[30]

A growth of traditional industry was observed not only in South Korea, but also in China and in the new industrial countries of East Asia, which to a significant degree followed the South Korean model. A peculiarity of the Korean case, however, was the fact that the rapid growth of production was accompanied by simultaneous growth in employment and by a rise in the technological level of industry, as well as by an increase in real wages. This served to refute the theory that new technologies automatically create unemployment. Despite rapid population growth, the demand for labour power in South Korea exceeded supply throughout the whole period of the 1960s and 1970s. 'As the economy grew at a fast pace, many unskilled workers were hired which helped to close the gap between supply and demand in the industrial market', the *Korea Times* notes. 'With an average economic growth rate of over 10 per cent, in the late 1970s there was a turnabout in the labor policy from job creation to protecting and improving working conditions.'[31] The number of workers employed in manufacturing industry almost doubled between the 1960s and the 1990s. Employment in other sectors of the economy also rose substantially. But, far from declining, the proportion of industrial workers among hired workers in general actually increased. The growth of employment in industry cannot, of course, continue at such a rate, and during the 1990s the proportion of industrial workers even began to fall a little. However, it is obvious that the traditional industrial proletariat is playing an important role in South Korean society, and that its organizational and political opportunities will therefore increase as well.

The forecasts of an uninterrupted decline in the role of industry in Western societies are not being borne out either. As a rule, such processes cannot be linear. Writers who try to extrapolate today's trends for another twenty or thirty years simply reveal their own methodological bankruptcy. It is quite obvious that the decline in the weight of industrial workers within society depends not only and not so much on 'objective' laws of technological development as on economic and social mechanisms. Industrial employment is indeed declining, but to an even greater degree it is being restructured.

In the mid-1990s more and more white-collar jobs were being lost. The automation of banks and service enterprises meant that fewer and fewer clerks were needed, while more and more technicians were carrying out essentially the same functions as their colleagues in industry. Researchers observed that the myth about the transformation of the services area into the main motive force for economic growth was based to a significant degree on its technological backwardness compared with industry. At the same time as industry cut its workforce through the rapid introduction of new technologies, 'white-collar productivity grew only slowly or even declined'. By the mid-1990s, however, firms had 'learned how to use information technologies to reduce the number of white-collar and middle management jobs. That is what downsizing is about.'[32] The relationship between industry and services was again changing, this time to the advantage of industry.

In traditional industry, where the first wave of the technological revolution had already passed by the beginning of the 1990s, the job cuts in the course of the decade have not been as sharp as in the 1980s. In the mid-1970s General Motors employed 500,000 people. In 1995 the corporation produced the same number of cars in the US using the labour of only 315,000 people. This is a substantial reduction, but nothing like the forecasts of the theoreticians of total automation, especially if we consider that elements of the productive process were simply handed over to outside contractors – that is, outsourced. Chrysler by the mid-1990s relied on outside contractors for 70 per cent of its components, and the same trend is evident with other corporations.[33] It is noteworthy that, as production is decentralized, jobs are not only being transferred from the developed to the developing countries, but are also being redistributed among the developed capitalist countries. 'If you buy a Pontiac Le Mans from GM for, say, $10,000', writes Canadian researcher James Rinehart, '$3000 goes to South Korea for assembly labor; $1750 to Japan for engines, transaxles and electronics; $750 to Germany for styling and design; $400 to Taiwan, Singapore, and Japan for small components; $250 to England for advertising and marketing services; and $50 to Ireland and Barbados for data processing.'[34]

Production is more and more dispersed, but it is impossible to get by without the blue collars. The traditional industrial worker still remains one of the key figures in the modern economy. This is acknowledged by many theoreticians of post-industrial society. D. Bell writes that post-industrial technologies cannot displace industrial or even agrarian ones, but merely add a 'new dimension' to them.[35] These various technologies often coexist, adding to the complexity of society.

As they set out to prove that the industrial working class is doomed, postmodernist writers often compare it with the dinosaurs that were doomed to disappear in the process of evolution. If history consisted of the replacing of old forms by new ones, this would indeed be so. But neither natural, nor social, nor even technological history develops according to this logic. The spread of the new does not by any means signify the disappearance of the old. All that changes is the relationship of forces and the distribution of roles between them. It is far from true that all the species that inhabited the earth in prehistoric times have vanished without trace. The dinosaurs died out, but crocodiles survived and found a place in a world populated by mammals.

Something similar is happening with industry as well. Its role in the world has changed. The traditional sectors will no longer serve as the motor of economic growth in most of the developed countries. The working class will no longer be the most massive class in society (although on the world scale it has never had this distinction). But this does not mean that it has no future. The survival and development of the working class in a changed society is just as natural as the survival throughout the twentieth century of a multi-million-strong peasantry, of the urban petty bourgeoisie and even of artisans, whom the theoreticians of the Industrial Revolution (including Marxists) consigned to oblivion more than a hundred years ago. Although the number of farmers in industrial countries has diminished, their political clout has remained quite significant, and to some degree even increased. This has happened not only because farmers have become more organized, but also because agriculture still plays a huge role in the industrial and post-industrial economy.

The persistence of the industrial working class in post-industrial society might be called 'the crocodile phenomenon'. Old technologies and the people who are expert in them are absolutely essential for the reproduction of new ones. Economists note 'a continuing demand for the kind of middle-level skills which, a generation ago, provided so many Americans with a comfortable living wage, whether machinists to build aircraft and turbines, or plumbers and electricians to construct and maintain homes and office buildings'.[36] The demand for these skills is even increasing. All that has stopped rising is the wages paid.

Proletarianization

It is curious that while sociologists speak of the disappearance of the working class, more and more people in Western society itself consider themselves part of this class. Data from a survey published in the *New York Times* in 1996 showed that when asked 'Which class would you say you were in?', 55 per cent of Americans answered 'working class' and only 36 per cent 'middle class'; 6 per cent assigned themselves to the lower class. Among the people who considered themselves to belong to the middle class, 35 per cent were afraid of falling out of it.[37] In earlier times the majority of Americans, including blue-collar workers, were inclined to place themselves in the middle class. But those days have passed. A sort of re-proletarianization is occurring, and also to some degree a marginalization of the middle layers. The exploitation of hired labour has grown more intense in virtually all sectors of the economy. 'The new hire-and-fire labour market made even the middle class terribly insecure about their jobs and future earnings, a fear which is wholly justified', observes Will Hutton.[38]

The technological revolution of the late twentieth century has passed through the same basic stages as the Industrial Revolution of the nineteenth century. The experience of recent years forces one to recall the lessons of industrialization in the nineteenth century. The large-scale introduction of machines at that time led to a dramatic weakening in the positions of organized manufacturing workers. The old unions and guilds were destroyed, but modern trade unions rose up in their place. As the industrialization of European countries proceeded, more and more new centres of the labour movement appeared. It was in the countries where industrialization occurred relatively late that a new experience of radicalism was accumulated.

By the mid-1990s the first stage of the technological revolution was drawing to a close in the main sectors of the economy. The productivity of labour and the potential of equipment will grow further, but this is now evolution and not revolution. The transition from the manual processing of data to computer processing amounted to a thoroughgoing revolution in the organization of labour. The transition from the 386 processor to the 486 or Pentium is simply a normal technical process, like the replacing of machine tools, such as has occurred throughout the history of industry.[39]

A natural consequence of the technological revolution on the world scale is the proletarianization of the 'free professions', and the rise of a 'new technological proletariat' often employed outside traditional industry. Often, the people themselves do not yet fully understand their real social status, especially since their position is extremely contradictory. This appears with particular clarity in the former communist countries. The Russian researcher Gavriil Khromov paints a discouraging picture of the psychological state of the scientific proletariat of the 1990s:

> They do not own and are not entitled to own their institutes, even if it made any economic sense for them to do so. They are denied the very possibility of influencing the character and fate of modern science; this is done for them by the scientific *nomenklatura* and by the state. They are defenceless on the social level, especially now that big cuts in scientific work are

> clearly impending, and there is no longer anyone who can complain to the authorities.[40]

While describing the psychology of scientific workers, Khromov also notes some striking contradictions. An openness to innovation is combined with the conformism that is essential if scientific workers are to create favourable conditions for their work and careers, while critical thinking is combined with political passivity. In terms of their economic position these workers are proletarians; in their ambitions they are 'unsuccessful petty bourgeois'; in their lack of civic commitment they are lumpens; and in their level of education and specialized knowledge they are 'the intellectual elite and heralds of the future'. The same applies to the ideology of the 'scientific proletarians':

> In line with the nature of scientific work, they are internationalists and westernizers; they have always taken a sceptical attitude to the idea of patriotism, which has struck them as too narrow a framework for the goals of their own lives. Now they are faced with another disappointment: international science, of which they have been used to feeling or imagining themselves a part, is turning away from them with indifference – turning away from the ageing and impoverished scientists of a chaotic country with a destitute science that is now of little interest. In better times, Russian scientists themselves looked on colleagues from Third World countries with the same condescending indifference.[41]

It is easy to see that the changes of the late twentieth century have had a disorganizing impact both on traditional and on post-industrial workers. The former have lost their self-confidence, while the latter are swiftly losing their privileged, elite status. Alienation and false consciousness are the quite natural results of people's inability to adapt themselves to new conditions. But such a state of affairs cannot continue indefinitely.

Following the devaluation of traditional skills and the growth of unemployment, the demand for labour power is reviving on a changed technological basis. The trouble is that the new jobs mostly come with lower pay, and sometimes with a lower level of professional education as well. Simon Head notes:

> Already in the 1990s the US economy has achieved a high rate of productivity growth, an even higher rate of growth of investment in information technology, and the creation of over eight million new jobs. But these successes have been achieved without any noticeable improvement in the nation's systems of vocational and high school education.[42]

There is nothing surprising in this. The growth in the educational level, skills and wages of workers during the industrial epoch did not take place automatically either. Just like technological progress, it was the result of changes taking place in society. To a large degree it was the result of the struggle by workers themselves for their rights, and also of political demands that had taken shape within civil society. It is enough to recall the role which in Marx's view was played by British factory inspectors, who forced the industrialists to limit their exploitation of labour power.

As industrial technologies spread, the significance of workers in society is increasing, and their class consciousness is growing stronger. Many processes typical of Western Europe in the early twentieth century are being repeated. But it is impossible to step into the same river twice. The failures of the European trade unions and of the left forces that have tried to mechanically reproduce ideas and actions that have never led to success are the best proof of that. It is in the process of overcoming setbacks that the movement can create new organizational forms and develop new leaders.

The world of labour has seen major changes since the time of Marx, but these changes have not amounted to the 'disappearance of the proletariat' surmised by fashionable sociologists. They do not even include the replacing of the traditional industrial worker with a hired employee of a new type. During Marx's time the world of labour was relatively homogeneous. This is why in the classical texts the concepts of the 'proletarian' and the 'industrial worker' are synonyms. Lenin, it is true, spoke of the cook who would have to learn to run the state, but it is scarcely likely that he had in view here the growing importance of the sphere of services – the European industrial worker was not simply a key figure for the theoreticians of classical Marxism, but the only one worthy of attention. This working class consisted mainly of white males, irreligious but schooled in the traditions of Christian culture. The rise in the early twentieth century of a colonial proletariat did little to change the general image of what a worker was like. Europeans for a long time were quite unwilling to recognize 'real' workers in representatives of the native populations. This was the case, for example, in South Africa: 'British workers, while often militant, never looked upon the non-white sector of the working class as allies, but as a threat to their own privileges.'[43] Despite the fact that the black proletariat performed the same functions, whites did not perceive it as part of the working class. From this came the scandalous slogan, heard during mass protest actions by workers in the 1920s, 'Workers of the world unite to keep South Africa white.'[44]

For their part, non-European workers who assimilated the lessons of the class struggle at first tended to reproduce the traditions, culture and organizational forms of the Western labour movement. The situation is now quite different. It is not the proletariat that is vanishing into the past, but the classical concept of it.

Analysing the global expansion of capitalism, Immanuel Wallerstein is even inclined to assert that proletarianization on a world scale is not only failing to disappear, but on the contrary is growing at unprecedented rates.

> The paradox is that these central processes of capitalist development as described by Marx, and which in turn account for the material and social polarization of the world, have come about not because of but despite the will and interests of the bourgeoisie as a class. It is the low level of proletarianization, not the high level, that has created and preserved the profit-making potential of capitalism as a system. It is the low level of bourgeoisification, and not the high level, that has created and preserved the political structures that ensured its survival. Neither proletarianization nor bourgeoisification are of intrinsic interest to capitalists.[45]

The globalization of the economy and the victory of the West in the Cold War have led to the proletarianization of the worker masses on an unprecedented scale, meaning that the appearance sooner or later of new 'antisystemic movements' is inevitable.[46]

The picture, however, is rendered dramatically more complex by the fact that proletarianization does not automatically mean the creation of the proletariat as a class of hired workers in the Marxist sense. The majority of the workers who have been drawn into the capitalist economy during the last quarter of the twentieth century are semi-proletarians. Moreover, this intermediate state is not necessarily temporary and transitional; it is supported and reproduced by the system. It is here that the reasons for the weakness, inconsistency and contradictory nature of many anti-systemic movements must be sought.

Informal Work and Traditional Sector

The world of modern-day labour is complex, heterogeneous and hierarchical. The degree of complexity is growing with every new step in the technological revolution. In the world today there are fewer European than non-European workers, while in the Western countries themselves the number of workers who are members of Third World nationalities is growing fast. There are almost as many women among hired workers as men. Depending on the technological level of production, workers may have quite different living and working conditions, and different requirements for the reproduction of their labour power.

Finally, the rapid growth of the informal sector has enormous significance for the modern economy. The millions of people who are engaged in informal and often illegal economic activity are just as essential a part of the world economy as yuppies from Wall Street. But there are substantial differences here as well. In the countries of Latin America and in the United States the boundary between the formal and informal economies is more or less obvious. The people who work in the informal sector are the unemployed and the marginalized. In the countries of the former Soviet Union this boundary has been eroded, and the same people operate in both sectors.

Social development is becoming just as multi-layered as economic development. Both the modernized and the traditional sectors have their own processes under way, often proceeding in parallel. Each sector is experiencing its own social differentiation, and provides the setting for the development of distinct ideologies and forms of political organization.

The growing complexity of the economy also gives rise to a number of new contradictions within the world of labour itself. The American researcher Norma Field writes of 'the polarization of the global workforce into elite, high-stress work at the top and sweatshop labor at the bottom, leaving a growing middle to be un- or underemployed for more and more of its life'.[47] Conflicts of interest arise between workers in the modernized and traditional sectors, and between skilled and unskilled workers. 'When skilled labor is released because of rising imports', writes the American economist Lester C. Thurow, 'skilled workers simply bump down the job distribution, knocking those with lesser skills out of their best jobs'.[48] Both sides ultimately lose, but the problem does not become less real as a result. The effective redistribution of incomes among workers depending on the sector or enterprise proceeds in just the same fashion: 'Those fortunate enough to work for a high-productivity team (a good firm) are paid more than those with identical skills who work on a low-productivity team (a poor firm). The lucky collect rents.'[49]

The less regulated the labour market, and the weaker the trade unions, the more acute such contradictions become. The tendency for wage scales to become levelled out, a tendency that appears in any capitalist society where there is a strong labour movement, also acts as a powerful stimulus to technological innovation, since it robs the entrepreneur of the chance to extract additional profit from the difference in the price of labour power within the sector. However, the contradictions that arise from the heterogeneity of the labour scene must inevitably result in disagreements among trade unions and workers' political organizations. During the 1960s and 1970s this was particularly evident in the countries of Latin America, with their multi-layered economies. In the final years of the century the same tendencies are to be observed in Western and Eastern Europe.

In industrialized Russia, the traditional sector is coming to include not only agriculture but also industry, which lags behind world levels. Unlike the situation in Mexico or India, a marginal in Russia is not a person forced out of the traditional sector and unable to find a place in the modernized one, but a worker in an industrial enterprise that is itself being marginalized as a result of a chronic shortage of investments, the collapse of the market infrastructure and the absence of any prospects for growth. This type of marginalization occurs even in areas that employ the most modern technologies. The traditional layers in Eastern Europe thus represent not a pre-industrial but an early industrial culture. Industrial traditionalism is becoming a very important element in mass consciousness in the West as well, as it is discovered that technological revolution does not replace old production with new, but merely creates a new hierarchy, devaluing workers in the 'old' sector and creating the conditions for their more intensive exploitation.

From the point of view of the class interests of hired labour, it is quite unimportant where most of the workers are concentrated, whether in industry, in the service sector or in scientific institutes. In the service sector the level of exploitation is even higher. The appearance in the US of massive numbers of cheap service jobs against a background of declining numbers of expensive jobs in industry speaks for itself. However, these differences are extremely important from the point of view of the ideology and organization of the labour movement.

On the political level, the contradiction between traditional and post-industrial labour is expressed in the schism between the old and new left. While members of the old left are demoralized and are losing confidence in the future, adherents of the new left are disoriented, and lack a clear strategy. Possessed by the idea of renovation, they are generally unable to develop a political programme and ideology that can ensure a firm bond with workers of the traditional sector. Since massive layers of post-industrial workers are still only coming into being, these workers are characterized by a false consciousness that is re-transmitted and reinforced by the contradictions and confused arguments of the ideologues.

Just as the new forms of labour cannot totally supplant the old, the new left culture has no chance if it arises as the negation of the old. On the contrary, the task of the left politicians and ideologues is to achieve the integration of the great traditions of the labour movement with the new trends that are becoming increasingly evident as the turn of the century approaches. The political and economic programme of historical socialism must not be rejected by the left movements of the new epoch, but on the contrary, needs to be built into a new, broader and more complex context.[50]

If post-industrial society, as imagined by its ideologues, has proven to be a chimera, there cannot be any question either that traditional industrialism has vanished into the past. Late capitalism both confirms the most important conclusions and forecasts of Marx, and at the same time gives rise to new facts, new contradictions and a new social experience not reflected in any way in classical left theories.

The increasingly complex structures of labour mean that the labour movement itself, its principles of organization and its methods of activity all have to change. This is a genuine problem, answers to which have to be provided not by post-modernist or even Marxist sociology, but by the experience of real struggle.

The new epoch demands that leftists carry out another rethink of their role in society. The politics and ideology of the left have to be aimed at helping to integrate the world of labour. Shared interests have to be identified and common demands formulated. Here we are not talking about a mechanical vanguardism, that subordinates 'backward' layers to the goals and tasks of 'advanced' elements. On the contrary, what is involved is a complex search for mutual understanding, since 'advanced' layers always finish up paying for their social egoism.

The terms 'industrial worker' and 'proletarian' are no longer synonyms. This means that it is necessary to reject the primitive workerism that has characterized socialists since the early twentieth century, and to return to Marx's original concept, that linked the future of society not simply with industrial workers, but with the proletariat in the broad sense of the word.

The historical working class could not have come into being without the experience of political and trade union organization, without the ideological work of the propagandists of socialism who had an enormous influence on the class culture, way of life, consciousness and, ultimately, even on the organization of labour. It is the idea of hegemony, Lenin wrote, that 'transforms the totality of factory workforces into a class'.[51] A class does not remain unaltered throughout the course of its development. The point is not only that the proletarian of the late twentieth century is different from the proletarian of Marx's time, but that the formation of the 'traditional industrial proletariat' was also preceded by a lengthy period of evolution. This proletariat did not instantaneously become the social formation that we find described in the socialist textbooks. The multitude of representatives of workshops and trades did not immediately become conscious of themselves as a class, did not immediately discover shared interests and develop a common consciousness. It was the process of political and organizational unification that created the working class as we know it from history.

Studying the process of formation of contemporary political parties, Gramsci came to the conclusion that from time to time the need arises to 'free the economic movement from the fetters of traditional politics'. Often, the changed needs of the masses contradict their traditional slogans. On the basis of these needs, a new 'historic bloc' arises.[52] The industrial proletariat became such a historic bloc in the late nineteenth century. It was only after having recognized itself as a class that the industrial proletariat managed to unite broader social layers around itself. It was not by chance that the ideas and even the organizational forms of the labour movement proved so attractive to the intelligentsia, the petty bourgeoisie, the peasantry and sections of the middle layers.

Ultimately, the differences between the work of coal miners, steel workers, seafarers and mechanics are almost as great as the differences between the work performed by any of them and that of workers in the post-industrial sector and the service area. It is the experience of social conflicts and joint struggle over many years that has caused the traditional working class to feel itself to be a united whole, and to place its common interests above narrow professional distinctions. The changes that have occurred in the social and employment structure of society could not fail to undermine this hegemony. The new structure demands that workers make new efforts to organize themselves. In a sense, it is necessary to begin anew the work performed by socialists, labour activists and trade union leaders a hundred years ago. It is essential to identify common interests and to assert their primacy over narrow group concerns.

A new historic bloc is now being born. It is broader than the traditional working class, but represents the historical continuation of this class. As Gramsci rightly noted, 'similar' social forces 'can merge into a new organism only on the basis of a series of compromises'.[53] In other words, nation, party, organization and class are always the fruit of compromise, of a complex process of fusion and mutual absorption, even if they themselves are not conscious of this. The reorientation of the left in the early years of the century, when it came to understand the need to unify the multi-million-strong masses of rural and urban 'semi-proletarians' around the working class, had enormous historical significance for the development of the labour movement. The communists, who proclaimed the slogan of the unity of the working class with the working peasantry, the social democrats, who declared themselves the 'party of the people', and radical national liberation movements standing for the defence of 'the oppressed', and not only of hired workers, all expressed this tendency in their own fashion. Without such a broad bloc the workers would scarcely have achieved substantial social progress. The bourgeois revolutions would not have occurred either if the bourgeoisie had not acted as the core of a broad popular bloc including the entire third estate. The peasantry could not have overcome feudalism independently, and the traditional working class was powerless to go beyond the bounds of capitalism. But the anti-feudal revolution could not have occurred without the peasants. Overcoming capitalism (and even substantially altering it) is impossible without the participation of industrial workers.

The world of labour today is not just 'objectively' disarticulated. For it to become a united social force, a unifying politics is required. If this politics is to come into being, there is a need for left organizations that have overcome not only the stereotypes of the classical past, but also the opportunist temptations of the present.

4

New Technologies, New Struggles

The history of modern computer technology serves as an excellent illustration of the classical Marxist thesis of the contradiction between the forces of production and productive relations. Efforts to turn information into a commodity and to distribute it according to the laws of the market clearly retard development and lead to numerous conflicts. Among the manifestations of the contradiction involved here is 'information piracy'. Combatting this phenomenon is in principle impossible, since any user of computer technology is drawn into it to one degree or another. The main centres of computer piracy are Russia, Bulgaria, Turkey and China, where unlicensed programs make up 90 per cent of those in use, and also Greece, the Czech Republic, Hungary and Yugoslavia, where the level is 80 per cent. However, there is also a demand for pirated programs in developed countries. In Germany, according to the Business Software Alliance, the corresponding figure is 50 per cent; in France 57 per cent; in Great Britain and Finland 43 per cent; and in Switzerland and the US 35 per cent.[1] As many as 94 per cent of the computer programs that change hands on the Russian markets are pirated. Not only are pirated copies to be had cheaply or free of charge, but they often include changes that make them more convenient for users than the originals. Early in the 1990s the program *Volkov Commander* appeared in Russia; this essentially reproduced the American program Norton Commander, but incorporated some very useful additions. Often, pirates Russify American programs, or translate them into other non-Western languages. The same happens with computer games. At one computer exhibition in Moscow visitors were shown a pirated version of the well-known game *Doom* in which the monsters cursed using Russian obscenities.

Pirates!

The liberal newspaper *Moscow News* lamented that 'in Russia, piracy is not regarded as anything dishonourable', and that the software producers themselves 'are not always interested in protecting their rights'.[2] The trouble is that many programs would simply not achieve mass distribution without the help of pirates. Not only is piracy responsible for creating tens and perhaps hundreds of thousands of new jobs throughout the world, but it also creates additional demand for programs.

Despite protests from Western software firms, the mass of users in Russia and many other countries clearly prefer the products of pirates. Microsoft and other Western corporations complain of multi-million-dollar losses, but this does not prevent these firms from being highly profitable. Experts note that profit rates in the sector can be as high as 80 to 90 per cent, which 'covers all the losses suffered by producers as a result of piracy'.[3] Even in Russia, where licensed copies of any program have until now been rare, Microsoft had a turnover in 1995 of about US$12 million. Russian software producers also achieved highly respectable incomes.

Also significant is the fact that, according to the leading Russian economic weekly *Ekspert*, until the mid-1990s not a single producer of computer software launched a court prosecution in Russia over breaches of its rights, although there was ample evidence of such violations. In 1996 Microsoft brought a number of suits against firms trading in computers, but all these cases ended in agreements on collaboration. As *Ekspert* noted, this could not be explained by shortcomings in the legislation. 'By mid-1993 all the basic laws affecting intellectual property were in place ... The quality of these laws was fully in line with world standards.'[4] It was only in late 1996 that Microsoft brought a number of prosecutions, including against unlicensed firms that had installed three-year-old versions of MS-DOS in computers![5]

The complaints by Western computer monopolies about Russian, Bulgarian and Chinese piracy are less than sincere, to say the least. Let us begin with the methods used in calculating 'losses'. Representatives of the firms estimate the number of their programs bought by users from pirates, calculate how much profit they would have made if all these programs had been acquired legally, and on this basis work out how much they have 'lost'. In reality, most of these programs could never have been sold at the official price. This is not only because the users lack money, but also because the firms themselves often lack developed dealer networks and market infrastructure in particular countries.

When the struggle against computer piracy began in Russia in the mid-1990s, one of the specialist journals in Moscow published an angry letter from the arctic city of Norilsk:

> I see the matter in simple terms. The pirates provide me with programs, while the producer firms, including Russian ones, don't provide me with anything. From their point of view, I should wait until they come and start flashing their mirrors and rattling their beads, trying to entice me and other 'natives' down from the trees where we've climbed after turning savage from waiting, and after leaving the message 'All Rights Reserved' on our computers as an epitaph.[6]

The executives at Microsoft understand this situation perfectly. It is no accident that this super-monopoly, as it penetrates markets in new countries, first shows a demonstrative indifference to the pirate copying of its products. This is because it is the pirates who create the primary structure of demand. If it were not for them, the firm would have to spend enormous sums introducing its products to the market. The pirates annexe new territories. Free of charge, they advertise the trademarks of leading firms, and accustom users to particular standards. It is only after the pirates have done their work that Microsoft unexpectedly remembers the losses it has suffered. Statements begin appearing in the press, and court prosecutions are launched. Similar strategies are used by other, less well-known companies.

In Eastern Europe the peaceful coexistence of Western firms and pirates came to an end in 1993 and 1994. In Russia the struggle between them is only beginning, because the market is far from conquered, and the risks associated with pressing ahead into the wilderness are as great as ever. But the first volleys in the trade war have already been fired.

Even after the primary market structures have come into being, piracy does not prevent the official producers of software from making huge profits. The production of computer programs follows laws quite different from those that govern industrial production. In industrial production, costs fall somewhat as the scale of output increases, but producing each new item requires additional quantities of labour and raw materials. With software nothing of the sort happens. There are no additional costs apart from those involved in producing a compact disc and recording information on it. The disc is cheap and the program is dear. The buyer spends money not for the disc, but for the program; he or she pays not for the commodity, but for the right to use it. The same also applies to telephone lines and electronic mail; from the moment the line is installed, the costs of the firm that installs it do not rise in proportion to the intensity with which it is used. The costs rise only for the client.

The economist Aleksandr Buzgalin notes that on the scale of society as a whole the defence of intellectual property is irrational. Society has an interest in keeping the direct and indirect costs associated with receiving information as low as possible. In theory, the producers of programs share this interest. 'The wider the demand for my information product, the wider the circle of its users, and the greater the number of people among whom I can distribute my costs, the lower will be the "price" of this new knowledge.' However, the mechanism for the distributing of costs is unacceptable to corporations that defend their exclusive rights over intellectual property.

> These mechanisms are irrational, since they involve huge additional direct and indirect costs: for the purchase (each time at the full price, and not on the basis of the distribution, and hence reduction, of the specific costs) and for the protection from copying and so forth of information products. This mechanism appears still more irrational if we reflect that the product of general labour in this case is not simply information; it is a *cultural value* ...[7]

In essence, what is involved here is not commercial profit, but a sort of monopoly rent. By refusing to pay it, pirates and their purchasers create a competitive market where one does not exist. But the firms do not lose out either. In order to maintain the system that allows them to receive rent from legal users, they must also put up with the unavoidable costs of piracy. The fact that the pirates must constantly be held in check is a quite separate matter.

The propaganda war against piracy is waged on several fronts. In the first place, we members of the public are told that stealing is wicked, and that when we buy pirated products we become in effect receivers of stolen goods. One of the authors of the anti-pirate articles that flooded the Russian press in 1995 and 1996 even claimed to see in the actions of pirates a social and ideological threat to the capitalist order. In his view pirates were ruled not only by the urge to enrich themselves, but also by feelings of 'protest against injustice' and by 'an instinct of universal collectivism, either inborn or inculcated by society'.[8] By an odd coincidence such articles began to appear in the Russian press after Western firms had decided that the Russian wilderness had been tamed sufficiently, and that it was time to move from peaceful coexistence with pirates to imposing order in the new market. Microsoft, together with other companies, established special prizes for good articles against piracy. Police actions also began to be mounted against traders in unlicensed programs. 'The results of the anti-piracy campaign', admitted one of the initiators, the entrepreneur David Barenboim, 'are known to all and recall the figure for profits in a well-contrived balance sheet: not quite zero, but close enough.'[9]

The majority of users in poor countries simply have no alternative. Sermons about morality are as useless here as attempts to forbid a starving person from taking a piece of bread without permission. Even Western journalists admit that licensed programs are simply not within the means of people in Russia or China, where a family may have to put aside money for years in order to buy a computer.[10] Moreover, everyone understands that, as a matter of principle, the dissemination of knowledge does not occur on the basis of the laws of the market. The notion of 'intellectual property' contains an inherent contradiction; knowledge is the only product that you can pass on to another person at the same time as retaining it yourself. In this area, the question of what belongs to whom is very contentious. It is enough to recall the scandal-ridden lawsuits that are fought out between the computer firms themselves, as they accuse one another of theft. For example, the firm Stac Electronics took Microsoft to court and won, alleging that the operating system MS-DOS 6.2 contained borrowings from Stac's software. Here it should be noted that the Russian laws have certain advantages over the Western ones. In the West, the legislation is oriented above all toward defending the interests of the vendor firms. In Russia the stress is on protecting the interests of the programmers and developers.

> If in the US it is customary to emphasize copyright ... in Russia the stress is on the rights of the author; that is, the primary right to commercial use lies with the author, who is free to retain this right or to cede it to another person. Hence according to the Russian legislation the company Microsoft cannot have author's rights by definition; it has only the rights to commercial use.[11]

The second front in the propaganda war involves references to the link between piracy and the epidemic of computer viruses. In practice, everything once again turns out to be far more complex, and cases are constantly being reported in which viruses have appeared in licensed products. No one knows exactly where the viruses came from, but one of the most popular versions has it that they were first created by the sellers of licensed programs as a weapon in the struggle against pirate copying.

Finally, the firms cite the additional services and other advantages which users receive from authorized dealers. This point is fair enough, but the users might well prefer to pay the market price for particular services, instead of a monopoly rent to the owner of knowledge.

Geopolitics of Knowledge

Since funds for the struggle against piracy are practically non-existent, the protection of intellectual property inevitably rests on prohibitory legislation. There is an obvious contradiction between protecting property rights in this sphere and protecting human rights. Any person who copies a program for a friend can be said to have become a computer pirate. New technologies make it possible for home computer users to copy not only diskettes but also compact discs, and to send programs by electronic mail. In order to prevent this spontaneous and massive piracy a system of total surveillance would be needed, along with strict controls over the movement of information. In some countries police already conduct 'searches' of computers whose owners are suspected of using unlicensed programs. The widespread use of such practices would constitute an unprecedented invasion of private and intellectual life (who knows what information about you might be found in your computer along with the unlicensed programs) and of the privacy of correspondence, as well as effectively putting an end to the sanctity of the home.

The problem of piracy also has another side, in this case geopolitical. The largest software firms are found in the countries of the capitalist centre, and most of them are American transnational corporations. Meanwhile, it is by no means the case that the programmers who work for these firms always receive 'Western' wages. In the computer industry as in any other, transnational companies extract super-profits by exploiting cheap, skilled labour power in the countries of the periphery. In the mid-1990s about 99 per cent of the on-line data bases containing scientific data and information on the technology of management, production, medicine and education were located in the US. While surrendering everything else, including the production of microprocessors, to Korean, Spanish and Japanese firms, the American corporations are trying to develop the production of knowledge at home. In Russia at the beginning of the 1990s all the socio-cultural conditions were present for the country to begin living off the production of knowledge in the space of five to ten years. But this fact in itself is still meaningless; the decisive factor is that of economic and political power.[12]

A monopoly on software is also a means of economic and political control, a form of support for the dependency of the periphery on the centre. According to data from the Russian Ministry of Foreign Trade, Russia each year loses about $500 million 'as a result of the uncontrolled export from the country of scientific knowledge and computer programs'.[13] Most of what is exported is used by American firms. This amounts to roughly half of the sum which American corporations claim to lose in Russia as a result of piracy.

Piracy, at least in the form of organized mass production and as an alternative system of distribution, is developing primarily in relatively poor countries – China, Bulgaria and Russia. The journal *PC Week* notes that Russian pirates rarely distribute copies of programs from their own country, preferring to 'plunder the ships sailing under the stars and stripes'.[14]

In a certain sense the struggle of today's computer pirates against large Western corporations can be compared with the resistance by English and Dutch pirates to the international dominance of Spain in the sixteenth century. Undermining the world monopoly, these seaborne pirates created a new geostrategic situation, and ultimately prepared the way for the appearance of a more just, free and open society.

It is no accident that the US government regards computer piracy as a strategic challenge, or that it is prepared to struggle against it using all the power of the state. The Chinese authorities, meanwhile, have not gone so far as to defend their own pirates, but are not showing any special zeal in combating them. Every time the pressure from the West is stepped up, the Chinese authorities declare that they are doing 'everything possible to defend authors' rights, patents and trade marks'.[15] In 1996 the US government vowed to impose sanctions on Chinese goods. Beijing in turn mounted a demonstrative campaign against piracy, destroying more than 20 million pirated compact discs, bringing 18,000 court prosecutions and shutting down a number of enterprises. But despite these measures, the scale of pirate production has continued to increase throughout the 1990s.

It is quite obvious that the Chinese state still has ample powers of repression. However, it does not see defending American intellectual property as one of its prime tasks. Nor does the struggle against piracy arouse enthusiasm in the law enforcement bodies of Russia; spokespeople for these bodies more and more often ask the question: 'Why should we use the money of our taxpayers to increase the tax base of Western states?'[16]

The declarations of the Chinese authorities to the effect that they are incapable of coping with pirates are just as insincere as the letters which Elizabeth I of England sent to the Spanish king describing the measures she was taking against sea marauders. The Chinese authorities understand that software piracy is opening the way for their country to enter the world of information technologies. Meanwhile, the cooperation which is developing spontaneously between pirates in Eastern Europe and China is laying the basis for a distinctive new economic order. Master copies are made in Russia, mass production takes place in China and Bulgaria, and the sales markets encompass all the former communist bloc. This is a highly integrated and decentralized 'common market'.

It is quite clear that computer piracy is not in itself a solution to the problem. Total victory for the pirates would lead to the collapse of the whole system of software production. The right of program developers to receive a decent wage has to be guaranteed, and the normal functioning of firms has to be ensured; this would be impossible if the software they produced was used free of charge by any and everyone.

The paradox lies in the fact that the way out of the problem is not to struggle against piracy, but against the system of which piracy is one of the results. Relations based on monopoly rent have to be replaced by relations of mutually beneficial cooperation. The point is that most users of licensed programs only buy them because they want to obtain the latest product. There is clearly a need to limit the right to the commercial exploitation of programs to a definite period (say, one and a half years). The norms of authors' rights that have existed since the nineteenth century presuppose just such an approach.[17] If this were done, a substantial proportion of pirated software would be legalized. Widely used programs would become just as much common property as the classics of world literature. Another solution to the problem would be compulsory licensing. Present-day Russian laws give the state the right to require this, stipulating that the decision should be made by the Supreme Patent Board – which the state, with typical Russian negligence, has simply forgotten to set up. Compulsory licensing would not by any means amount to state piracy, since the producer would receive compensation or royalties. However, this would mean the end of monopoly rent.

What would in fact be involved would be the socialization of the software market. Software libraries could be established by the state and municipal authorities, with access open to all, in the same way as ordinary libraries were set up in the past. A small subscription charge or 'computer tax' would make this system self-supporting. Meanwhile, the state would assume the role of an intermediary, supplying the mass of users with cheap, good-quality programs on a completely legal basis. The world-wide computer network, the Internet, is evolving in the same direction.

The Struggles in Cyberspace

The Internet does not function according to the laws of the market; rather, it exists on a basis of communist principles, since it belongs to no one and to everyone. The costs of maintaining the system are justly distributed among its users, and everyone benefits from it according to their needs and abilities. In the global sense the Internet and modern-day information technologies mean the beginning of the end of market capitalism and the abolition of private property in the form which it has historically assumed. 'Intellectual property' is a contradiction in terms. The ownership of knowledge (something closely asociated with privilege, inequality, dictatorship and censorship) is vanishing into the past, but authors' rights remain, as do the mutual obligations of participants and the need for cooperation. Predictably, the Internet has become not only a global information network, but also a knot of contradictions. On the one hand, there are efforts to impose censorship within it. It is typical that American, Russian and Chinese legislators are trying at the same time to bind users of the Internet with various restrictive and prohibitive measures. In China since 1996 the government has forced users of electronic networks to send their messages only through special ports and filters controlled by the authorities. Special systems for the filtering and censorship of electronic mail have been developed by Saudi Arabia, Bahrain, Iran and Vietnam. France is trying to limit the use of the English language in the 'national cyberspace', while in the United States, Germany and Japan legislators are waging a constant struggle against 'indecent' materials in electronic networks. If the restrictions in Western countries are being introduced in order to further the struggle against pornography, and in the East mainly to limit the flow of political information, in Russia restrictions are being sought just in case. In 1996 the State Duma drew up a draft law containing a detailed list of 'types of information, allowed to be transmitted abroad'. Since such restrictions would immediately be violated, it was proposed to set up organs of control which among other functions would unmask 'untrustworthy, false, foreign documented information'.[18]

After the Zapatista Army of National Liberation (EZLN), headed by Subcomandante Marcos, used the Internet to help organize an international meeting in the Mexican state of Chiapas, the liberal Moscow weekly *Itogi* informed its readers that the Internet was becoming an arena of revolutionary struggle. 'Today the governments of the largest industrial powers are sounding the alarm because of the limitless communication possibilities of the Internet as a tribune for destructive antisocial forces', reported the terror-stricken journalist. Computer networks in the hands of radicals, he considered, were more dangerous than Stinger missiles in the hands of insurgents. The wide distribution of computers makes them especially dangerous. 'Concealing information will be even more difficult, and disseminating it easier. The computer experiences of Subcomandante Marcos will go down in history as simply a trial run for the "Internet commandos", winning battles with the authorities without shedding blood.' Furthermore, 'because the Internet assumes the absolute "equality" of any information that you put into the network, computer *samizdat* is much more effective than *samizdat* on paper, for the simple reason that it is much harder to outlaw'.[19] The inference is that in order to save the values of the free world, it is essential to introduce harsh censorship of electronic networks, and to ensure total control over access to them, day and night.

In Russia, hostility to the Internet unites government bureaucrats with ideologues of the opposition. In 1996 the newspaper *Zavtra*, which is close to the leadership of the Communist Party of the Russian Federation, published a programmatic article setting out to prove that the computer poses a threat to humanity.

> The entire twentieth century can be understood as a process of the ever-greater invasion of our lives by various technical devices without which we can now no longer get by. It is as though a healthy person were gradually, over many years, trained to walk on crutches.

If technical progress is in principle evil, then from the point of view of the ideologues of Russian patriotism the computer is doubly malignant. 'Every computer taken separately is no more than a single cell, dangerous only for its immediate owner. The real danger is posed by computers joined in networks, especially if the networks are global.' In the Internet, rootless cosmopolitans are transformed into virtual ones. They rummage about in our data bases, study us and implant their ideology. 'A computer addict', we are told, 'develops a dependency like that of a drug addict, and the more unstable the person's psyche, the stronger the dependency becomes'. With the help of the Internet, 'worldwide forces operating behind the scenes' (and it is in precisely this fashion that the leadership of the Communist Party describes the source of all Russia's ills) turn our children into miscreants. 'What will a young neurasthenic who spends six to eight hours a day shooting terrifying virtual monsters (something that is no longer unusual) eventually grow up to become? A Russian daisy or cornflower, or an American cactus, a murderer?'[20]

It is of course far from true that technical progress brings only good in its wake. However absurd the technophobic attacks of *Zavtra* might be, they are in essence a continuation of a quite natural tradition of criticizing progress, a tradition which began as far back as Rousseau. The trouble is, however, that even the most irreconcilable enemies of progress will not agree to return to the stone age. Proof of this is to be found in the newspaper *Zavtra*. On the very same page where the article on the harm done by computers was published, the Internet address of that esteemed journal was to be seen displayed.

The horrors of total surveillance and of a general manipulation of consciousness that are described by the patriotic press could well become real, although neither police controls nor the deception of the masses can exactly be called recent innovations. The problem is not in the technology, but in the question of who uses it and how. The Internet that is opening up new possibilities for humanity, is also becoming an arena of fierce struggle.

Against the background of a government policy of control and filtration, large Western monopolies (once again, primarily Microsoft) are persisting with efforts to turn the Internet into an arena for their expansion. Enthusiasts for the Internet have discovered that this may turn out to be a far more serious danger than the obviously doomed attempts at information censorship. After the state ceased to regulate the Internet and it was opened up to commercial information, it began growing rapidly. Since 1988 the number of subscribers to various Internet services has doubled every year, and on some international lines the volume of information transmitted has doubled every four months. At the same time, elements of chaos have appeared in the network, and the problems have multiplied. An 'administrative vacuum' has appeared.[21] Journalists have argued about who should impose their control and 'bring order' to the Internet – the state, the telephone companies or Bill Gates's Microsoft.

> The Internet has been a model of what can be achieved through the combination of public funding and innovative

> technology. Today, it is being transformed into an electronic shopping mall and sales catalog. And it is only a matter of time before many of the Internet's most useful attributes disappear in the wake of commercialization.[22]

This pessimism is excessive. The Internet is capable of digesting powerful streams of commercial communications. The world of the market will not succeed in overwhelming the world of information, because in this latter world the laws are different. The only way order can be maintained in the network is on the basis of free association. A far greater danger for the network lies in the efforts to control people's access to information on the pretext of defending 'intellectual property'. The British economist Alan Freeman is convinced that the policy of defending intellectual property represents the most serious threat to democracy since the time of the Holy Alliance, established by European monarchs for the purpose of combating the French Revolution.

> For the first time since Metternich, it is a crime to share information. There are associations and crack police teams who can enter any house or company in search of forbidden information and jail people for having it. In negotiations on 'free' trade, point number one is the restriction of information flow.[23]

The struggle for the right to the free exchange of information shows the degree to which democracy, on the threshold of the new century, has become inseparable from socialism. Knowledge is becoming the basis of production and of prosperity. As UNESCO expert Philippe Queau observes, neo-liberal policies aimed at privatizing knowledge and at turning it into a source of private profit represent a clear infringement of the 'right of the public to information'.[24] These policies are in conflict with the ethical norms that have spontaneously been established in the Internet. Efforts to transfer bourgeois norms to the network, dividing users into rich and poor, meet with spontaneous resistance.

In 1996 one of the ideologues of the Internet movement, John Perry Barlow, published his 'Declaration of the Independence of Cyberspace'. Addressing the powerful of the world, he declared:

'Your legal concepts of property, expression, identity, movement, and context do not apply to us. They are based on matter. There is no matter here.' The spread of the Internet and of new technologies constitutes a challenge to the old order.

> Your increasingly obsolete information industries would perpetuate themselves by proposing laws, in America and elsewhere, that claim to own speech itself throughout the world. These laws would declare ideas to be another industrial product, no more noble than pig iron. In our world, whatever the human mind may create can be reproduced and distributed infinitely at no cost.

In sum, the Internet is becoming the basis for a new social order, an alternative to the present one:

> We are creating a world that all may enter without privilege or prejudice accorded by race, economic power, military force, or station of birth. We are creating a world where anyone, anywhere may express his or her beliefs, no matter how singular, without fear of being coerced into silence or conformity.[25]

At about the same time the Moscow journal *Hard'n'Soft* published a declaration entitled 'Our Proletarian "No!" to the Technophobes of the Earth'. Here the authors called for the defence of 'virtual reality' from incursions by the authorities, security services, mafias, bourgeois and 'pseudo-intellectuals': 'There is nothing that remains for us to do except to defend ourselves. For this, however, there is absolutely no time left.'[26]

Resolving the contradictions that are arising as a result of the development of the global information space does not require prohibitions, but laws aimed at defending the interests of program users and developers. But their interests are counterposed to those of the large Western firms that profit from the sale of intellectual property.

Transforming information into a commodity serves in practice to undermine the bases of the market economy itself. The British researcher John Frow drew attention to this when he noted that, according to liberal theories, the normal functioning of the market requires a maximum of information openness, while the concept of 'intellectual property' demands the restricting and regulating of access to information. This contradiction not only explodes many of the dominant theories, but also affects the practical work of enterprises. 'The profit structure of the markets directly undermines the basis of the market system itself.'[27]

The rule of private property also retards the development of hardware. 'The "inter-departmental" barriers that have spontaneously arisen in the information space come increasingly often into conflict with the technological norms of mass production, and artificially limit the capacity of the channels of free commodity exchange', writes Yuriy Zatuliveter in the journal *Hard'n'Soft*.

> While carrying out laborious and extremely complex tasks, the developers of technology and programmes are forced to repeat one another in most of their functions. This significantly lowers the efficiency with which the labour and qualifications of these workers are employed. Facing an excessive variety of choices, and with extremely vague criteria for making them, consumers are in practice limited to a few more or less similar alternatives; consumer choice is thus held in check. The impression arises that the 'Tower of Babel' of the computer world was designed and built by the most powerful firms for the sole purpose of extracting profits.[28]

The rule of big capital leads not only to the monopolization of the market by a few large companies, but also to a situation in which technological standards that are far from the best available are imposed on computer users.

> The principle of spontaneity does not allow the computer market to make the transition to a new qualitative basis in a rapid and straightforward fashion. Widespread trends are now appearing for hardware and programs to become unified. These trends reflect the advantages of one or another set of technical solutions or organizational measures, imposed de facto and consolidated through mass production. Only the most powerful firms are capable of proceeding along this path. The negative side of this process is the growth of concentration and of the conservative influence of the computer monopolies; this makes it extremely difficult for promising but

> 'heretical' ideas to survive, while increasing the opportunities for the self-interested manipulation of users. The use of coercive methods for establishing and maintaining standards 'de facto' requires constantly growing expenditures, but there are limits to everything.

The classic conflict arises between social needs and private interests. The need for standardization and integration contradicts the logic of private property, profit and free competition. A situation arises which is very like that which existed with the railways in the early twentieth century. 'Under conditions of mass production the contradictions that are accumulating in the dispersed information space cannot be solved by natural means', Zatuliveter reflects. 'The only way to save market mechanisms of production and consumption from being overwhelmed by unavoidable contradictions is by creating a single, unified information space, which must first of all come to include the computer hardware and software industries.' Only then, Zatuliveter maintains, will the development of technology be subordinated not to the interests of the 'moneybags', but to the 'fundamental laws of information'.[29] These laws presuppose general access, equality and common ownership of 'new values'. In sum, Zatuliveter argues, 'it is possible that the computer world is preparing to take a historically irreversible step toward the socialism that has until now remained out of reach'.[30]

Many Western economists are coming to analogous conclusions. Even in traditional areas of production, the conditions for change are ripening.

> Excessive consciousness of property rights on the part of firms may undermine and prevent potentially productive strategic alliances and cooperative relations. The blurring of inter-firm boundaries both among competitors-cum-allies and between clients and their privileged single suppliers inevitably entails a loss of control over intellectual capital. Similarly, technology transfer, conceived as investment in congenial organizational ecology, directly involves a sharing of knowledge among potential competitors; it is therefore typically impeded by excessive property consciousness.[31]

Overcoming excessive property consciousness with the help of sermons and recommendations from management specialists is impossible. Attitudes to property will change of their own accord if property relations change. This is a question of politics, of a struggle of interests – a struggle that is only just beginning.

5

The New Periphery

When the Berlin Wall came down in 1989 and the countries of Eastern Europe flung themselves into the embraces of the West, No one wanted to think of the problems and trials lying ahead. Three years later, when the Soviet Union had disintegrated and the Russian Federation that had arisen on its debris proclaimed its determination to carry out a transition to capitalism, everyone knew that the changes would be painful. That was clear from the experience of the former fraternal countries of Central and Eastern Europe, as well as from the fact that the Soviet economy had been in a state of serious crisis from which there could be no escaping without losses. But neither in 1989 nor in 1991 were there large numbers of people who doubted the correctness of the course that had been chosen, or that ultimately, the triumph of capitalism was guaranteed. Along with capitalism, it was agreed, would come an efficient economy, freedom and prosperity. A few diehards protested, but no one paid them any attention.

Ten years later, there were fewer and fewer people in the former communist countries who retained this faith. The ideologues of neo-liberalism, whether imported or home-grown, promised the people of Eastern Europe that their countries would merge with the West. After ten years, living standards in the two parts of the continent have not come any closer together.

From Hope to Frustration

The countries of Eastern Europe first experienced a profound economic decline. Some of them later achieved a certain growth, but none managed to surpass their pre-crisis levels, let alone reduce the gap that separated them from their Western neighbours. Recognizing that they would not achieve success on their own, the countries of the former communist bloc are now tying their hopes to integration with the political structures of the West. As was the case ten years ago, the plans of the elites enjoy broad support in society. Everyone thinks that entry into the NATO military alliance or the European Union will finally allow these countries to escape from the impasse in which they find themselves, and really to join the family of rich nations. Political integration, it is assumed, will draw economic integration in its wake.

> When living standards decline for most of the population and corruption cases undermine domestic support for the ruling parties, progress reports about European integration appear a source of legitimacy for government policies. 'Europe' has been elevated to a position of ultimate authority from which the policies of reform and transition, including all austerity measures, can be derived from agriculture to banking.[1]

Leftists have propagandized in favour of entry into the European Union no less actively than rightists, seeing in this a chance 'for the development of the social state'.[2]

These hopes are doomed just like the earlier ones. Membership of NATO has not brought wealth to the people of Turkey, and there is no way it can improve the position of the masses in Poland or Hungary. Where the European Union is concerned, the countries of Eastern Europe have encountered unthinkable bureaucratic obstacles. They are being called upon to furnish data on a multitude of indices inconceivable even to Soviet planning specialists. They are being forced to coordinate all sorts of trivia, right down to the diameter of a tomato. In fact, there is something far more substantial behind the bureaucratic delays than a desire by bureaucrats in Brussels to extend their pleasure in the exercise of power. The West simply cannot integrate Eastern Europe, even if it wanted to. The hopes for an improvement in the social situation in the East following unification with the West are at best naive. If the eastern countries ever enter the European Union, this will sharply alter the union's character. From being a club of the elite, it will be transformed into a hierarchical structure through which the poor and weak are bound to the will of the rich and powerful. In short, the structures of an 'expanded' West would be doomed to become something like the Soviet bloc structures that were destroyed in 1989 – and perhaps, something considerably worse.

Seeking integration into the Western structures at any price, the former fraternal countries are acting according to the principle 'everyone for themselves'. The Czech Republic, Poland and Hungary are forcing aside Romania, Slovakia and the Baltic republics. Ukraine is trying to arrange a place for itself toward the end of the queue. Russia no longer has any chance. The traditional ties that existed in the region long before the arrival of Soviet forces have been drastically weakened, while the contradictions have grown more severe. Accordingly, the countries of the region are becoming increasingly dependent on the West for everything, from technology to information. Yugoslavia once prided itself on its independence of military blocs and its freedom from acute inter-ethnic conflicts (except for the problem, which made its effects felt periodically even under Tito, of the Albanian minority). Today the former Yugoslavia is not merely a territory wracked by ethnic warfare, but is gradually being transformed into a zone of NATO military action.

Ever greater masses of people are realizing that the course chosen in 1989 is a dead end. As a result, protest movements are gripping one country after another. In 1998 and 1999 popular disturbances have shaken Albania and Romania. The authorities have had to use armed force to suppress the discontent. But even that has not helped. Bitter clashes between workers and police are becoming commonplace in Poland and Ukraine. The political life of the region is being transformed into an endless train of crises.

However, it is not only the admirers of Western capitalism that have finished up in a difficult position. Their left-wing opponents also face serious problems. In 1989, when no one doubted that capitalism would triumph in Eastern Europe, Marxist critics of the system were convinced that the new social relations would quickly force the working class to recognize where their real interests lay, to organize themselves, and to defend their rights. In other words, the development of capitalism would provide a powerful stimulus for the renovation and rise of the left, just as occurred during the nineteenth century in the West.

In the decade from 1989 to 1999 this did not happen anywhere except in Eastern Germany. The reason was not simply that socialist ideas were discredited; public opinion surveys show that in practically all the countries from Mongolia to the Czech

Republic these ideas have become significantly more popular than they were in 1989. The customary explanation for the weakness of the left, 'leadership sell-outs', cannot be regarded as satisfactory, since efforts during the years from 1989 to 1999 to found an honest and principled left opposition – and there were many such attempts – also ended in failure. The picture is almost the same, whichever country one examines. Eastern Germany remains the sole exception, but it is an exception that brilliantly confirms and illuminates the rule. The eastern Lander, seized by western German capital and officialdom, were on the one hand openly colonized – which could not fail to arouse protest – and on the other hand were integrated politically into a stable democratic system, becoming the poorest and most exploited part of a rich society.

Transition and History

To understand what happened in the other parts of Central and Eastern Europe, it is necessary to delve into the very essence of the capitalist development that has occurred here. During the ten years since the fall of the Berlin Wall, Eastern Europe has not simply rejected communist slogans and privatized state enterprises, creating its own financial oligarchy. It has also become part of the world capitalist economy – its new periphery.

All the traditional features of a peripheral economy are present. Debt dependency, that had already become a serious problem for the communist regimes in the 1980s, increased rapidly in the 1990s, when the communists were replaced by liberals. Dependency on foreign markets and technology increased, and the informal economy expanded. A shortage of capital, to meet the growing need for modernization of obsolete equipment, became a general problem of all the economies of the region. All the countries of the former Soviet bloc inherited a substantial industrial potential from the previous regimes. Even taking account of the fact that the efficiency of production and the quality of the products were invariably below Western levels, this potential was impressive compared with other regions of the world. It was precisely this fact that was the source of many illusions about successful future development.

Meanwhile, the few investments that the region succeeded in attracting were of little benefit to its industries. Analysing the priorities of investors, the Hungarian economist Jozef Borocz notes three guiding principles: '(1) interest in real estate development predominates over industrial production; (2) investment with the purpose of penetrating the Hungarian and/or East-Central European market predominates over production for core markets; and (3) evidence of the re-emergence of some pre-war linkage patterns.'[3]

Not only did the year 1989 fail to mark the end of history; it was not its beginning either. No one can begin with a clean sheet. Prior to the Second World War the countries of Central and Eastern Europe, with the exception of the Czech lands, were the periphery or semi-periphery of the West. National capital was weak and dependent on foreigners, state structures were authoritarian and officials were corrupt. It was the weakness of Eastern European capitalism that explains the inability of the local elites to resist the German onslaught in the years from 1939 to 1941, and the subsequent inclusion of these countries in the Soviet sphere of influence. Throughout the period of existence of the communist bloc, Eastern Europe was forced to wear the strait-jacket of the one-party system, but at the same time it underwent rapid modernization. Poland, Yugoslavia and Hungary were rebuilt from ruins. Cities and industries sprang up, and systems of universal education and health care were created. For the lower orders of society, opportunities that had been completely lacking in earlier times were opened up. When political crisis enveloped almost all the countries of the Soviet bloc following the death of Stalin, a solution was found through combining repression of active opposition with internal reforms that improved the position of the majority. This decision proved highly effective. Living standards rose continuously until the mid-1970s. A consumer society took shape in Eastern Europe. Meanwhile, the scope of individual liberties grew steadily broader. The anti-communist ideologues of the 1990s prefer to forget how harsh the political regimes in most of these countries were before and during the Second World War. Compared with these governments the communist regimes by the 1970s could even be seen as more liberal, at least in Hungary and Poland. All this provided a certain mass base for the communist regimes, which were not by any means kept in power exclusively by Soviet bayonets. In the Soviet Union itself the political system was becoming increasingly lenient, allowing people to hope for further gradual progress.

The modernizing potential of the Soviet system, however, had clearly been exhausted by the end of the 1970s. This occurred earlier in some countries than in others. In the USSR economic growth rates began falling as early as 1959, when postwar reconstruction was essentially completed. Czechoslovakia, which suffered least during the war and which had possessed the most developed economy in pre-communist times, was the first country to find it no longer had any prospects for development within the framework of the existing system. This was why, in 1968, the movement for reforms in Czechoslovakia was supported and even initiated by a significant section of the party–state elite. However, the Soviet Union itself was not ready for changes. Moreover, the oil crisis that hit following the 1973 Arab–Israeli war sent a powerful stream of petrodollars flowing into the USSR. At the same time, cheap Soviet oil spurred a continuation of industrial growth in the 'fraternal countries'. Under Leonid Brezhnev, the main slogan in the USSR became 'stability'. This stability was purchased at the cost of refusing to seek new paths of development. Under the new social pact, the population would refrain from calling for increased civil freedoms, and in return would receive increases in consumption. This was a time of growing corruption, not only at the top, but in all layers of society. The oil dollars paid for imported consumer goods and technologies. However, this money was insufficient, and the Soviet government began resorting to foreign loans. The 1970s were a time of cheap credit. As a result, Poland, Hungary, Romania and the Soviet Union came to figure among the largest debtors to the West.

The road of development that had been chosen ensured that the countries of Eastern Europe would increasingly be drawn into the world economy, as the periphery of the West. Their dependency increased steadily throughout the 1970s and 1980s. At the same time, their internal problems were not being solved. From the point where the system proved incapable of satisfying the consumer expectations which it was itself calling forth, it ran up against growing political dissatisfaction, multiplied by narrow-minded resentment. The movement of 1989 was just as much an uprising by enraged consumers as it was the revolt of an awakened civil society.

The result was the collapse of the communist regimes in Eastern Europe in 1989 and in the USSR in 1991. However, the change of regime did not by any means signify a shift in the general direction of development. Meanwhile, the removal of the structures of communist power served precisely to open the road to the final transformation of the countries of Eastern Europe into the periphery of the capitalist world system. In this sense, the years from 1989 to 1991 were neither a turning point, nor the beginning of a new epoch, but merely saw the culmination of processes that had developed over the preceding decades.

It is this which explains the astonishing ease with which the communist elites yielded power. They themselves had long felt weighed down by this power, or more precisely, by its previous form. Of course, the bureaucracy was not united. Its ideologues and its repressive apparatus feared change, but their influence was no longer especially great. The relationship of forces differed from country to country; Czechoslovakia saw its 'velvet revolution', while in Romania things reached the point of civil war. The degree of participation by the masses in the process of change also differed. In Poland and Romania the people came out onto the streets demanding change, in Hungary they passively awaited the results of a 'round table' of the authorities and the opposition, and in Russia a substantial part of the population was wary of the reforms from the very beginning. Nevertheless, the overall dynamic and social nature of what was happening was the same everywhere. The old *nomenklatura* solved its own crisis at the price of destroying the system. The *nomenklatura* sought to retain its positions, converting power into money, so that with the help of this money it could hold on to power. The communist elite had begun turning bourgeois long before 1989. The disintegration of the eastern bloc allowed it to openly proclaim itself a bourgeoisie.

On the surface, it might seem as though the events of 1989 were a continuation of the reformist efforts of 1968. But this was not so. In the course of the 1970s the bureaucracies underwent substantial changes. The Brezhnev period was the time when the ruling layer in all the countries of the Soviet bloc became totally corrupted. Paradoxically, this corruption made the bureaucracy receptive to the slogans of democracy. The new needs that had arisen among the elite could be fully satisfied only in an 'open society'. In addition, there was a need for a new mechanism for the legitimization of authority. In circumstances where society was becoming increasingly stratified, an egalitarian ideology no longer suited the people at the top, since it could not serve as a justification for their rule.

This is why the slogan 'socialism with a human face' was everywhere quickly rejected. The convinced communists of earlier times readily became liberals or right-wing social democrats. In Czechoslovakia and to some degree in Russia, the participants in the movement of 1968 were forced into the margins of political life. Elsewhere, as in Poland, they were driven to radically change their ideology, following behind the party bureaucrats.

East Germany was an exception. It was simply annexed by the West. The consumer expectations of the masses were satisfied, but the local *nomenklatura* was forced out by the incomparably more wealthy and powerful Western bourgeoisie. After the bureaucrats had been dealt with, the local intelligentsia began to be subjected to oppression as well. The victims protested. These were active, educated, experienced people. Denied the opportunity to become integrated into the system, they were full of the desire to change it. It is not surprising that in the German 'new Lander' the left movement revived far more quickly than in the rest of Eastern Europe.

In the broad scheme of things, the masses were hoodwinked everywhere. But it would be just as correct to say that the people everywhere received precisely what they had demanded. The situation recalls the well-known tale of the man who wants to become rich in a single day – next morning he is told that his beloved son has died, and that he is to receive an insurance pay-out. In 1989, the people wanted freedom and access to Western consumer goods. They received both – but at what cost?

Capitalist Reality

The economies of all the post-communist countries experienced a profound depression, and living standards fell. For the bulk of the population access to education became more difficult, and the system of universal free health care was undermined. The consumer paradise turned out to be a club for a chosen few. Unemployment in all the countries except for the Czech Republic and Belarus reached the levels of 10 to 16 per cent.

Since neither the state nor private business was able to create jobs in sufficient numbers, people began living according to the principle 'saving the drowning is a job for the drowning themselves'. Millions of people were drawn into petty private business, but on an extremely low technological and organizational level, which as many scholars acknowledge, makes small business 'more of a brake than a "locomotive" of economic changes'.[4] These entrepreneurs are not so much a petty bourgeoisie as marginals, with neither property, nor reliable means of subsistence, and who keep themselves fed only with difficulty. Their lives are unstable, and full of shocks. By the late 1990s the proportion of self-employed in the countries of the former Soviet bloc, after quickly outstripping the levels of Western Europe, Asia and Latin America, was approaching that of Africa.

A rapid growth in the 'shadow economy' occurred in almost all the countries that underwent liberalization. It is curious that in 1989 the ideologues of reform invariably argued that the black market and illegal business flourished exclusively under conditions of central planning and strict state regulation, as an elemental reaction by society to 'unnatural' restrictions on economic activity. Practice has shown otherwise. The well-known Russian scholar Sergey Glazyev notes that 'removing the state as the main agent of control in the economy has not led to market self-organization and competition, but to organized bandits taking over this function'.[5]

Despite the demagogic promises of modernization, the economy and society in virtually all these countries have undergone precisely the reverse. Firms and institutions have been equipped with computers, but the educational level of the population has fallen sharply. The lag behind the West has increased. The indices for the efficiency of production have deteriorated even in the most prosperous countries, such as the Czech Republic. If the energy-intensiveness of the Czech economy in the late 1980s was about 40 per cent higher than in the developed countries of Western Europe in terms of energy use per head of population, and 150 per cent higher per unit of GDP, by 1995 this gap had increased. This was linked directly to the slowdown in the process of renewing equipment in the enterprises. The Czech Republic also lagged further behind the West in terms of the productivity of labour. In 1989 this index was 39 per cent of the level in the European Union, and in 1995, despite the modernization of a number of firms purchased by Western capital, only 33 per cent.[6] In other countries the technological lag, and dependency on the West, grew much more dramatically. In Russia and Ukraine the situation became simply catastrophic.

As in the countries of the Third World, a technological stratification of the economy has taken place. On one side are a small group of advanced firms, integrated directly into the world market, paying high wages, and owned by foreign capital or serving its interests. On the other side are all the remaining enterprises, trying to operate on the local market and having difficulty making ends meet. The paradox is that the 'advanced' firms would not last for a single day if the 'backward traditional sector' were not ensuring the self-reproduction of society as a whole. In reality, the foreign entrepreneurs and local finance capital, with active support from the authorities, are off-loading their costs onto the traditional sector.

Any unbiased observer will see that conscientiously following the neo-liberal prescriptions has not made a single country richer. 'Plucky Moldova and Kyrgyzstan followed the recipes of the International Monetary Fund cookbook to the letter, but their economies continue to sink resolutely', the American professor Peter Rutland states in bewilderment. 'In contrast, Slovenia refused to privatize, but due to circumstances of history and location enjoys the highest living standard in the region and is on the fast track for entry into the European Union.'[7] It suddenly turns out that everything is due to geography.

In reality, privatization has not only failed to assist in modernizing the economies of Eastern Europe, but has been closely linked to the overall decline in output. A marked growth of industry has occurred in precisely those countries that have not followed the dictates of the IMF – in China, where the communist regime has survived, and in Belarus, where after several years of crisis President Alexander Lukashenko, so detested by the West, came to power. A degree of success was also registered between 1989 and 1997 in the Czech Republic, where privatization was merely simulated (the privatized enterprises were bought up by state investment banks). The results of privatization in Ukraine have been particularly instructive. Analysing the results of liberal reform, economist Yury Buzdugan stated that the slump in output was invariably greater in the sectors where widespread privatization had been carried out.[8]

The abandonment of price controls and the introduction of complete freedom of entrepreneurship did not bring the promised well-being either. As early as 1994 Glazyev stated: 'In the degree of liberalization of its economy, Russia has outstripped many developed capitalist countries. However, our present freedom from state regulation and oversight is supplemented by freedom from responsibility for the methods and results of economic activity.'[9] The country was sinking into an unprecedented crisis. The fall in output exceeded anything seen in the Great Depression, and the financial collapse of 1998 also revealed the complete bankruptcy of the policy of financial stabilization. The crisis proved so deep, that in 1999 even moderate experts were stating that the only real way out of it lay in 'a shift to a mobilization economy'.[10]

The circle had closed. A policy aimed at dismantling central planning and state management of production had brought the country to a situation from which escape was simply impossible without emergency measures and active state intervention.

It is significant that falling economic growth rates and a growing technological lag behind the West are constantly cited as the main symptoms of the crisis that led to the downfall of the Soviet-type societies. After setting out on the capitalist path, over the next decade these societies endured a much more severe decline, and, at least on the surface, reconciled themselves to technological dependency on the West. The explanation is simple; what was unacceptable in the framework of competition between two systems became perfectly normal after the entire world was united in a single capitalist system. In the context of this system, it was quite normal that some countries should develop more dynamically than others, and that the backwardness of the periphery should be a necessary condition for the flourishing of the centre.

Of course, the countries of Eastern Europe themselves hoped to become part of the centre. In 1989 most of the citizens of the communist countries were profoundly indifferent to the fate of the people doomed to hunger in Africa or to poverty in Asia. The results of the reforms were not only predictable, but were also thoroughly deserved. The poverty and instability that have spread like an epidemic through Eastern Europe are a sort of historical retribution for irresponsible consumerist ambitions and racist contempt for the rest of the world.

If the promise of Western-style wealth was a deception, democracy to one degree or another became a reality. In this too there is a paradox; when people dreamed of a Western standard of living, they did so in private, but when they demanded Western political freedoms, it was out loud. Ultimately, they received precisely what they had demanded – freedom. But without wealth.

Institutions characteristic of Western democracy arose in virtually all the countries of the region, including even Albania and Russia. The question was: how would these institutions function in societies strikingly different from those of the West? In the Czech Republic and Poland, Western institutions have proven relatively effective, something that cannot be said of Albania with its rigged elections, of Russia with its authoritarian constitution, or of Latvia, where almost half of the population has not received the rights of citizenship. Even the most prosperous countries, however, have met with problems capable of putting a question mark over their democratic future.

The decade from 1989 to 1999 has been a period of global triumph for neo-liberalism. The collapse of communism in Eastern Europe not only strengthened the process through which these countries were being drawn into the capitalist world economy as a new periphery, but also allowed the strengthening of neo-liberal hegemony in the West and the Third World. The left was demoralized. For the peoples of the Third World, the ending of the Cold War, a development which in Europe was perceived as an enormous achievement, signified a return to the times of undivided economic and political domination by the West. In their turn the elites in the post-communist countries, who had been defeated in the Cold War, were ready to accept any terms from the victors. All these elites asked was that they could win integration into the capitalist system for their countries, and for themselves, a place in the global ruling class.

Nationalism: Myth of the Golden Age

The costs of the process of transformation were to be paid by the bulk of the population. For millions of people who had been awaiting the onset of the consumer paradise, this came as a shock. Not surprisingly, neo-liberal ideology in its pure form quickly lost its attractiveness. If the people were to accept further sacrifices, additional motivations were needed. Neo-liberalism was reinforced with nationalism.

In Eastern Europe, of course, nationalism was nothing new. Throughout the Soviet period, nationalist ideas had been a powerful stimulus impelling people to resist the regime. The nationalist interpretation of the history of Eastern Europe saw in communism nothing more than a system brought in on Soviet bayonets. The Russian nationalist press in emigration, by contrast, argued that communist ideas were profoundly alien to the Russian people; they had been imported into Russia from the West, and had been implanted mainly by Jews and Latvians.

In their search for a national alternative to communist theory and practice, the ideologues of nationalism turned to the years before 1945 (in Russia, to the times of tsarism), seeing in them a sort of golden age. From the very first, the regimes that succeeded the communists saw their goal as resurrecting the past. Hence the general restoration of old state symbols (as in Russia, Hungary and Poland), and at times also of the old constitutions (as in Latvia and Estonia). Poland and Russia, though formally remaining republics, embellished their coats of arms with crowns. In Slovakia, Croatia and, until 1996, in Belarus as well, state symbols that had earlier been used by local fascists were given official status.

The return to the past was always utopian. In all the countries of Eastern Europe the social, economic and even demographic structure of society had changed radically since the 1920s and 1930s. In some countries the national make-up of the population had changed as well. For Russians living in Latvia and Estonia, the transition to independence meant the loss of citizenship rights. In other post-Soviet republics people of non-titular nationalities simply began to be sacked from their jobs, while Russian schools were closed.

The idea of returning to a pre-war golden age was a reactionary one, since the existing society, after being transformed by 40 years of communist rule, was on a far higher level of social and economic development than the one to which it was proposed to return. It is not surprising that the further the process of restoration proceeded, the greater the spontaneous resistance became. Parents did not want compulsory teaching of the law of

God in the schools and kindergartens. Women were unhappy at attempts to limit their right to abortion, at more complicated divorce procedures and so on. In a number of countries of Eastern Europe restitution laws were adopted, providing for the return of confiscated property to its former owners. This resulted in the eviction of thousands of people from their apartments, and in the closure of museums and enterprises occupying buildings that had been 'seized by the communists'. In Romania, where property had been redistributed a number of times, several 'lawful owners' often made claims to one and the same plot of land. Disputes over the rights of property owners were accompanied by outbreaks of violence.

Meanwhile, the de-modernization of social life was linked inextricably to the pro-Western orientation in politics and the economy. This was quite natural. In pre-communist times most of the countries of Eastern Europe had been in a situation of unconditional economic dependency on the West. The return to the past was an ideology ensuring the restoration of the structures of peripheral capitalism. This thoroughly suited the transnational companies and the Western financial institutions. As for the local elites, most of them simply had no other choice.

The critics of neo-liberalism joined in blaming the new elites for trying to return society to the nineteenth century, and to implant in Eastern Europe a social order that had long since disappeared in the West. Comparing the capitalism that had taken shape in the east of the continent with the capitalism holding sway in the European Union, it was not hard to arrive at such a conclusion. 'The society which is in fact now arising in Russia is remote from the models in countries with highly efficient, socially-oriented market economies', states a report from the Russian Academy of Sciences:

> Rather, it is a society based on a hypertrophied property-owning stratum, on corruption, on organized crime, and on dependency on foreign countries. From the socio-economic point of view this is not a step forward, but amounts to throwing the country back by two hundred years to the epoch of a primitive, 'savage' capitalism.[11]

'In Poland today a wild capitalism of a nineteenth-century character has emerged', writes the Polish economist Tadeusz

Kowalik.[12] We are trying to reproduce obsolete models, and hence 'we are going about our lives back to front, constantly stumbling onto the inevitable', the well-known Russian commentator Viktor Gushchin writes indignantly.[13]

The idea of a 'savage', 'primitive' and 'backward' capitalism in Eastern Europe suits leftists and neo-liberals alike. It allows the former to refer calmly to classical Marxist texts, while the latter, by contrast, can argue that in the course of time or as civil society develops, Eastern European capitalism will also become 'civilized', just like in the West. In reality, both sides are profoundly mistaken. In Europe in the epoch of savage capitalism there was neither an International Monetary Fund, nor a developed system of stock market speculation, nor transnational corporations. The backward and savage Eastern European structures are intimately connected to the advanced and civilized Western ones. Moreover, Western capitalism in the 1990s has by no means been evolving toward a more civilized character. Trying to explain the processes occurring in the East by using such concepts as 'backwardness' and 'underdevelopment', or by referring to the costs of primitive accumulation, makes no sense at all, since the general principles of neo-liberal reform have been applied both in Eastern and Western Europe, as well as in the countries of the Third World and in the United States. During the 1990s, in other words, it is not so much that post-communist capitalism has become civilized, as that Western capitalism has become savage. The only difference is the fact that neo-liberal policies in the West have run up against the tight defensive ranks of the institutions of civil society. The bourgeoisie has been forced to conduct drawn-out positional warfare against the welfare state. By the late 1990s, with the adoption of the Maastricht Accord, the advent of the euro, and the founding of a European Central Bank independent of governments and the population, it might have seemed as though this struggle had been won – that the defences of civil society had everywhere been broken through, and that the bases of the welfare state had been undermined. Civil society was decaying before our eyes, turning into a commonwealth of consumers. However, this process had been going on for almost two decades, and the victory of the neo-liberals was undoubtedly Pyrrhic.

In the post-communist countries, where civil society was weak, the neo-liberal model could be imposed through a 'cavalry attack', that is, far more quickly and consistently. Despite the propaganda, the events of 1989 by no means represented the victory of civil society over the state, especially since the one cannot in principle exist without the other. Western-style political institutions were established, but, as before, participation by the population in political life was minimal and there was almost no connection between democratic procedures and the decision-making process. The Hungarian liberal commentator Miklos Harasti acknowledges that the handshakes that concluded the Hungarian Round Table of 1989 signified something more than a wish to carry through the transition to democracy in peaceful fashion.

> I personally cannot imagine any Western democracy where 15 consecutive years of falling standards of living would not have prompted a mutiny of populist sentiments, or the rise of extremist political adventures, or both. There has been nothing like that in Hungary, where the political class enjoys a surprising lack of competition from outside the original Handshake club.[14]

Post-communist democracy has turned out to be just as underdeveloped and backward as the local capitalism. But here as well, the problem is not a lack of traditions or a shortage of time. The underdevelopment and the backwardness both have a common explanation – after 1989, the societies of Eastern Europe were finally integrated into the capitalist world system, in the role of a periphery.

Of course, the position of the various countries in the system was not identical. The Czech Republic and Slovenia, like the German new Lander, were closer to the centre than Poland and Romania, not to speak of Russia and Ukraine. Not even the most favoured countries, however, have any chance of quickly becoming real parts of the West. The resources needed for broadening the 'club of the elect' simply do not exist. The possible success of the Czech Republic or Slovenia could mean new problems for Portugal and Greece, whose membership in the club is only tenuous.

Non-capitalist Capitalism

Peripheral capitalism develops according to a logic different from that of the capitalism of the countries of the centre. The notorious accumulation of capital, which is supposed to ensure the rise of a local entrepreneurial class, has turned out to be impossible, since within the framework of the globalized world economy a spontaneous redistribution of investment resources constantly takes place, to the advantage of the centre. By the end of the decade almost all the states of the former communist bloc were encountering the same problem as the developing countries of Africa, Asia and Latin America – a shortage of investment.

The theory according to which the triumph of private property would quickly give rise to a class of independent entrepreneurs has also been refuted by experience. 'The most distinctive characteristic of post-communist social structure in Eastern Europe is the absence of a capitalist class', sociologists state.[15] 'After six years of economic freedoms', the liberal writer Dmitry Galkovsky notes in astonishment, 'you can do little more than walk about the centre of Moscow with a lantern in broad daylight, calling out "Show me a real capitalist!".'[16] Galkovsky is echoed by Miklos Harasti: 'With few exceptions, it is the poor of communism that have become even poorer, and the powerful of the *ancien regime* who have become the new upper class.'[17] There is no reason to be surprised at this, since from the very beginning it has been the essence of the transition that has been under way since 1989. The *nomenklatura* has been bourgeoisified, but it has not become a fully fledged bourgeoisie. It has merged with the world capitalist system, accepting the rules of the system's game, but has not shed its own specific features. From the communist system, the *nomenklatura* and the technocrats inherited not only their contacts and power, but also to a significant degree their methods of rule. These methods have turned out to be perfectly compatible with privatization and liberalization, leaving both market ideologues and orthodox Marxists in an impasse. Can such societies be called capitalist at all?

Liberal researchers found analogous 'aberrations' in the countries of South-East Asia with their crony capitalism, and even in Japan, with its semi-feudal business structure. They decided with hindsight to explain all the failures of market economies by just such 'specific local features'. Meanwhile, peripheral capitalism cannot be other than distinctive and anomalous. Early in the century Rosa Luxemburg observed that capitalism, while including more and more countries in its orbit, did not destroy the traditional structures there completely. On the contrary, the traditional elites played a decisive role in the formation of the capitalist economy, providing it with access to new markets and cheap resources. Such a role has also been played by the post-communist corporative structures in Eastern Europe.

It is precisely the retention, to a significant degree, of the old order in society that has prevented a social explosion, despite the mass dissatisfaction with the course of 'reform'. The dependence of workers on management; the remnants of social welfare provisions, transformed into bureaucratic paternalism; and political clientelism have all provided an effective defence against class struggle. Real bourgeois property relations are always accompanied by real trade unions, real workers' parties, and so forth. And the danger of a real revolution. In this situation the elites are unable either to pay Western wages (this would result in local entrepreneurs immediately losing their competitiveness), or to maintain social spending at its previous miserly level.

Alongside the maintenance and development of corporative ties, a large sector of the workforce is also being marginalized. These masses are capable of rising in revolt, but cannot become an independent political force. Revolts occur constantly – now in Albania, now in Romania, now in Russia – but do not expand into revolution.

The communist system did not allow people to become conscious of their interests, or to unite in order to defend them. In the former society, the main way in which individual citizens acted independently was as consumers; everything else was organized for them by the state. This is why, in 1989, millions of people were so extraordinarily naive, and so easily allowed themselves to be manipulated to the detriment of their own interests. The market, by contrast, forces people to be conscious of their own interests, and of how these interests clash with those of other people. Workers discover that they are not only consumers, but also hired employees. The experience of the market is an essential school for all anti-capitalist movements. On this level, Lenin was correct when he stated that trade unions, by defending the economic interests of workers, act as a school of communism.

In such a situation, it is of vital importance for peripheral capitalism to maintain traditional bonds, defending workers from the shock of the market and sparing entrepreneurs a head-on collision with workers. However, these corporative, patriarchal and corrupt traditional structures are an obstacle to the creation of a more dynamic entrepreneurial class. They block the way to modernization even in the sense in which modernization is necessary to international finance capital. Society finishes up in a dead end.

Local liberal ideologues and Western commentators argue with hindsight that, as in the case of Indonesia, it is the traditional structures that are responsible for the failure of reform. These people call for society to rid itself of the local 'barbarism', and once capitalism has been 'cleansed', for the countries to be integrated into 'world civilization'. In exactly the same way, Gorbachev ten years ago was calling for the Soviet system to be cleansed of bureaucracy and authoritarianism. In terms of the ideology of neo-liberalism, Eastern European capitalism is just as deformed as Soviet socialism was in terms of the ideology of *perestroika*.

This contradiction gives rise to endless debates between 'Westernizers' and defenders of the 'native soil' (that is, nationalists) in virtually all the countries of the former eastern bloc. However, neither the supporters of the 'Western road' nor the champions of a 'distinctive identity' can suggest a real way out of the situation. They cannot even get by without one another, since in practice the civilized and barbaric structures are closely interconnected. In most of the countries of Eastern Europe the leftists have become 'Westernizers' (perhaps the only way in which they differ from the rightists), while in Russia, which has experienced a profound national humiliation, the Communist Party has turned to Slavophilism. In each case, however, the left parties are trying to base themselves not on the masses, not on the majority of workers, but on particular sections of the local elites. In effect, the leftists have become part of the neo-liberal system, unable and unwilling to act as expressions of mass protest. Even against this background, the nationalist policies of the Communist Party of the Russian Federation in the years from 1994 to 1999 have been scandalous. The problem has not only been the anti-Semitic utterances of its leaders. While in opposition, the party voted each year to adopt a monetarist budget. In 1999, while workers were going hungry in many parts of the country, and desperate health and education workers were taking to the streets, party leaders declared that political life in the country was 'losing its dangerously antagonistic features'. The party saw its task not as defending the interests of workers, but as uniting:

> the forces which make a stand for the priority of national-state values, which promote a strong economy oriented toward the welfare of the whole country, and which also defend the idea of the rebirth of a Russia which is great in all the roles it performs.[18]

What the bases of this economy might be, the party leaders preferred not to tell us. It was not surprising that even when society as a whole was shifting to the left, such a party could not strengthen its position, but lost ground.

From 'Resisting the Change' to Changing the System

In fact, everyone lost. After less than ten years, the sometime victors found themselves in the same trap as those they had defeated. Peripheral capitalism could not modernize Eastern Europe. For that matter, any serious attempt at cleansing capitalism using liberal formulas is doomed to the same failure as Gorbachev's *perestroika*. Destroying the corporative and *nomenklatura* structures without undermining the very bases of peripheral capitalism is impossible. Efforts to replace the *nomenklatura* pseudo-bourgeoisie and the criminal clans with 'real' entrepreneurs cannot succeed without placing the very principle of private entrepreneurship and 'the sanctity of private property' in doubt. This is why the question of modernization in Eastern Europe can be resolved only by the left, and only through radical anti-bourgeois measures. In the late 1990s not a single country in the region was ready for such changes, and the left parties themselves were incapable of acting as a radical force. There is only one conclusion that flows from this – in the absence of new revolutionary shocks, the post-communist world is doomed to continue along the same path it is following today.

This will condemn the peoples of the region to new sacrifices and disappointments. In such circumstances, a decay of political democracy is inevitable. All its symptoms can already be discerned. In practice, the making of real decisions is already remote from democratic procedures (something that can be observed in the West as well), while state institutions are becoming increasingly authoritarian, and nationalist movements are rising up from below.

How can this be resisted?

Opposition to the system is growing. Elements of the working class, passing through the school of the market, are being transformed into a potential mass base for left movements, although this base is incomparably smaller than orthodox Marxists have supposed. It is important to note, however, that the left can easily find itself allies. After rejecting the communist system, Eastern Europe is again faced with the same problems that have tormented it since the beginning of the twentieth century. The questions of modernization and independence, with which liberals, communists and nationalists have all failed to cope, are back on the agenda.

In this situation, leftists are obliged to put forward their own project. This project will be national, and at the same time consistently anti-nationalist. It will be national inasmuch as it is concerned with the country's own priorities of development, with how to overcome dependency on the West and to place the economy at the service of the country's own interests. It will be anti-nationalist because nationalism is the ideology of the local elites, who are interested in maintaining their privileges, and hence also in preserving peripheral capitalism. In the modern world, it is impossible to wage a struggle for national independence on one's own. The peoples of Eastern Europe have repeatedly shown solidarity in defending their rights against the Soviet 'big brother'. Solidarity is even more necessary when the place of the Moscow big brother is taken by the one from Washington or Brussels. Despite all the old resentments, there can be no hope of independent development without regional integration. In just the same way, the peoples of Eastern Europe will sooner or later have to abandon racist complacency and acknowledge that their historic fate has united them not with Western Europe and the United States, but with Latin America, Asia and Africa.

Integration with the European Union represents the last hope and the last great illusion of the Eastern European consumer. These hopes will not be realized either for those who remain outside the union or for those who are accepted. The former will not receive anything, while the latter once again will receive things they were not anticipating. The political cycle is reaching its culmination. The dreams of integration into the 'club of the rich' are being replaced by an understanding that one's own interests have to be defended. The consumer has to become a citizen and a proletarian.

The national project of the left also has to be anti-nationalist because it can rest only on a broad bloc that includes both various groups of workers, and also an important layer of technocrats who have an interest in changing the priorities of development. The ideology of 'ethnic solidarity', like that of the 'chosen people', is incompatible with the principles of democracy and labour solidarity. In Eastern Europe a single, homogeneous working class of the type described in the works of traditional Marxism does not exist. In essence, it does not exist anywhere. Under the conditions of peripheral capitalism, the left movement arises not as a class movement, but as a popular one. But, at the same time, even such elementary demands as calls for wages to be paid promptly or for the coal industry to be preserved place the very existence of the system in question. These demands cannot be satisfied until all economic relationships, including relations with the West and the IMF, undergo radical changes.

The crisis of the elites is also a crisis of the official post-communist left parties, which are closely intertwined with these elites. But at the same time, this crisis also provides an opening for a new left movement to appear. The way out of the existing situation is not through 'social accord', but through tough confrontation and the expropriation of the post-communist oligarchy, through radical structural reforms. National interests have to be counterposed to the interests of the elites. The local elites are anti-national in their essence, since they are anti-popular. Their nationalist rhetoric is merely a cover for their day-to-day plunder of the bulk of the population. Neither international nor local capital can carry out the tasks of social and technological modernization, for the simple reason that such tasks are not even on their agendas. Still less are they able to mobilize the resources needed for radical change. Any project of national development requires a dramatic increase in the role of the state as the key investor. This means that privatization must sooner or later be replaced by a policy of broadening the public sector.

No Way 'Back to the USSR'

The return of old problems inevitably brings with it the temptation to repeat old solutions. Does this mean that in Eastern Europe, or at least in some of its countries, a revival of the communist system that collapsed in 1989 is possible? Some people dream of this, while others fear it. But you cannot step into the same river twice. Despite the parallels between the end of the century and its beginning, there is a fundamental difference between these two periods. The Soviet years did not pass in vain. Society became far more educated, developed and complex. It is precisely for this reason that the orthodox communist grouplets trying to live by the formulae of the 1920s are so weak.

The left faces the task of drawing lessons from the history of Soviet communism, and also from the experience of national development in the Third World. In this case the problem is not how 'socialist' these models were. What is important is that both arose as alternatives to peripheral capitalism. Both suffered defeat. The countries of Eastern Europe returned to the capitalist world system, while the states of the Third World never broke out of it. But at the moment of its greatest historical triumph, this system itself has run up against its own insoluble contradictions. It is becoming more and more weighed down by crisis. Meanwhile, the countries that have become its periphery are receiving a new chance to break out of its vicious circle of dependency and backwardness.

Both the Soviet model and the national movements in the Third World provided accelerated development at the price of denying democracy. In the final analysis, this disregard for human rights and freedoms was the decisive reason for their defeat. Not so much because millions of people in 1989 suddenly began to want freedom (in reality, many of them did not even know what it was), but because an unfree society cannot mobilize its innovative potential, and cannot successfully resist the propaganda offensive and consumer blandishments of capitalism.

By the late 1990s it had become clear that the political liberation was simply a by-product of the crisis of the communist regimes. In its long-term perspectives, peripheral capitalism is incompatible with democracy. At best, democracy in this setting is a facade, mere window-dressing. A revival of the left in Eastern Europe (and in the world as a whole) depends ultimately on the degree to which leftists succeed in becoming the leading democratic and innovative force. First, the left has to propose a new model of the state and the public sector – open, dynamic and oriented toward carrying out the strategic tasks of development. The success of the left also depends on whether it can advance, as an alternative to globalization, a new model of regional integration, in which the various components enjoy equal rights and are free from the imperial heritage.

Will this new, liberating project be realized? Will it become part of broader global changes that lead ultimately to the abolition of the capitalist world system and its replacement with a more just world order? A real political struggle in the post-communist countries is still only beginning, and so far there are more questions than answers. One thing is obvious: there will be no special fate for the citizens of Eastern Europe after 1989. We will either win or lose together with the majority of humanity.

Conclusion

It was the Hallowe'en night of 1998 when the spectre of communism haunted New York City. About 1,000 people gathered in Cooper Union to celebrate 150 years of *The Communist Manifesto*. It was the same Cooper Union where 115 years earlier a crowd of American trade unionists and socialists gathered to pay tribute to Karl Marx after his death.

In 1998 the *New York Times* had to publish the news from Cooper Union on the front page of its Metro section and it got more coverage than the Hallowe'en parade which itself that year turned political. Though the *New York Times* reporter clearly did not like it, she had to accept the fact that 'Karl Marx, dead and buried for 115 years, can still fill a hall.' It was surprising and she looked for explanation:

> That the manifesto retains the power to move people with its confident prediction of capitalism's self-destruction may relate to its unfulfilled promise more than to the political movements that operate in its name. Or perhaps it is the poverty of political discourse these days or the habit of judging a society's well-being largely by the coughs and sneezes of its stock market.[1]

The real answer to the question about Marx being alive and well after so many years is that capitalism is alive. And capitalism is in crisis. After the crash of 1997 in Asia and the economic catastrophe of 1998 in Russia this is undeniable. It was not any socialist or radical journal but the *Financial Times* that published an article 'Das Kapital revisited', asking why the world had swung 'from the triumph of global capitalism to its crisis in less than a decade'.[2] One can hope that sooner or later things will improve because 'this is just a matter of time'. It is not. And this is not just a cyclical crisis. It is structural. And it is here to stay at least as long as we keep the global structures of the free market liberal capitalism unchanged. As Ken Livingstone wrote, 'The enormous shifts on financial markets are not driven by "psychology" or "herd mentality" but by absolutely fundamental international economic forces.'[3] After undermining the state as the agent of regulation, after defeating socialist challenges, global capitalist institutions (including multinational companies) discovered that they are not able to control the process which they themselves started.

The society has changed since the times of Karl Marx, no doubt about that. But how did it change? Many of the prophesies made by Marx were actually premature for his own time, but now they come true. Capitalism is now global. So is its crisis.

The simple truth is that Marxist analysis of capitalism is correct. But while this is becoming more and more evident to market analysts and managers this is not the case among socialist politicians.

The left remains hostage to its own failures and neuroses. It is not only weak politically but it lacks the determination and moral strength needed for action. It can win elections but not struggles. Unless it dares to speak again about class solidarity, nationalization and redistribution, unless it challenges the system of global capital and its local political representatives, it has no chance to change anything.

And with the crisis of capitalism becoming deeper, with democracies more and more divorced from real decision-making and global economic forces escaping control, the alternative posed by Rosa Luxemburg is becoming clearer: socialism or barbarism. Now we understand that this was not an exaggeration, not a poetic way of speaking about possible dangers. This is just the only real choice.

Leftist politicians, who do not dare to choose socialism and fight for it, will bear full responsibility for the possible outcome: the triumph of barbarism.

Notes

Preface

1. See M. Castells. *The Information Age: Economy, Society and Culture, vol. 1: The Rise of the Network Society*. Oxford, 1998, p. 6.

Introduction

1. *Links*, July–October 1996, no. 7, p. 74.
2. W. Hutton. *The State We're In*. London, 1996, pp. 23–4.
3. F. Fukuyama. *The End of History and the Last Man*. London, 1992, p. xiii.
4. Donald Sassoon. *One Hundred Years of Socialism*. London and New York, 1996, p. xiii.
5. Ibid., p. 649.
6. See D. Sassoon. 'Fin-de-Siècle Socialism: The United, Modest Left', *New Left Review*, January–February 1998, no. 227. This is Sassoon's Isaac Deutscher Memorial Lecture given on 2 December 1997. The very fact that Sassoon's book *One Hundred Years of Socialism* was awarded the Deutscher Memorial Prize reveals the scale of moral and intellectual crisis of the Western left in the 1990s.
7. *Korea Focus*, January–February 1998, vol. 6, no. 1, pp. 114, 113.
8. *PerForming Times* (Bulgaria), January 1997, p. 1.
9. L.C. Thurow. *The Future of Capitalism*. New York, 1996, p. 264.
10. *Shepherd Express*, 8 April 1999, p. 7.
11. *Quoted in Workers' Liberty*, February–March 1997, no. 38, p. 15.
12. See *Nezavisimaya Gazeta*, 6 March 1997.
13. *War Report* (Institute of War and Peace Reporting, London), November–December 1996, no. 47, p. 18. It is also important to note that the 'left-wing' Italian government remained among Berisha's main supporters even after the 1997 popular uprising.
14. See *Itogi*, 11 March 1997, no. 10, p. 24.
15. *Washington Post*, 20 September 1998.
16. *Moscow Times*, 15 September 1998.
17. *Financial Times*, 15 September 1998.
18. *Economist*, 31 October 1998.
19. *Moscow Times*, 17 September 1998.

1 The Left As it Is

1. *Moscow Times*, 18 March 1997. It is significant that in many cases voters have rejected moderate candidates, instead favouring more radical ones. In the 1997 elections in El Salvador the Democratic Party, established by two moderate organizations that split from the FMLN, suffered a total defeat.
2. *Links*, January–April 1996, no. 6, p. 27.
3. D. Sassoon. *One Hundred Years of Socialism*. London and New York, 1996, p. 759.
4. *Mapping the West European Left*. Edited by P. Anderson and P. Camiller. London and New York, 1994, pp. 99, 100.
5. *Correspondances internationales: informations et analyses sur le mouvement ouvrier et les forces de gauche dans le monde*. Ed. by P. Theuret. Paris, September 1995, no. 22, p. 20.
6. Ibid., p. 19. Here and subsequently the results of elections are cited from: *Correspondances internationales, informations et analyses sur le mouvement ouvrier et les forces de gauche dans le monde. Special élections européennes 1979–94. Resultats des forces de gauche et écologistes*. Ed. by P. Theuret. Paris, May 1995, no. 19.
7. See *Inprecor*, May 1997, no. 413, p. 16.
8. *Socialism and Democracy*, Summer–Fall 1992, vol. 8, nos 16–17, p. 123.
9. Ibid., p. 17.
10. See *PDS Pressedienst*, 18 April 1997, no. 16, p. 3.
11. *Rossiyskiy obozrevatel'*, 1996, no. 4, p. 132.
12. *Polis*, 1996, no. 4, p. 118.
13. *Rossiyskiy obozrevatel'*, 1996, no. 4, p. 132. In passing, it should be noted that reformism cannot in principle be evolutionary. The very need for reforms (that is, transformations, however moderate they might be) arises only when society cannot through its 'natural' evolution solve the problems that confront it. Reformism (if, of course, it is taken seriously) is methodologically compatible with revolutionism, but never with the ideology of 'natural evolution'.
14. N. Bobbio. *Left and Right: The Significance of a Political Distinction*. Cambridge, 1996, p. 78.
15. Quoted in *Le Monde Diplomatique*, March 1997, no. 516, p. 11.
16. *La Repubblica*, 22 Dec. 1996.
17. M. Weber. *Izbrannye proizvedeniya*. Moscow, 1990, p. 572.
18. *Voprosy sotsiologii*, 1996, no. 7, p. 189.
19. *Svobodnaya mysl'*, 1995, no. 8, p. 65.
20. D. Sassoon, *One Hundred Years of Socialism*, p. xxii.
21. The term 'deferred revolution' (*otlozhennaya revolyutsiya*) was used by L.D. Trotsky to refer to the state of Russia in the period between 1906 and 1914. I have used the same term in a

different context to explain the reformist character of the workers' actions in the West since 1918, when workers, without ceasing to be in opposition to capitalism, have not been ready to struggle for its revolutionary overthrow. It is this elemental reformism of the 'lower strata', and not the 'treachery of the political leadership' that, in my view, accounts for the failure of revolutionary alternatives both in the period between the world wars, and during the years of the Cold War. See B. Kagarlitsky. *Dialektika nadezhdy*. Paris, 1988.

22. Boris Frankel. *Beyond the State? Dominant Theories and Socialist Strategies*. London, 1983, p. 280. It is curious that this book, which contains a very harsh attack on all critics of traditional state socialism, was published by Macmillan Press in a series edited by Anthony Giddens.
23. W. Hutton. *The State We're In*. London, 1996, p. 24.
24. Ibid., pp. 262, 267–8.
25. The Russian economists Aleksandr Buzgalin and Andrey Kolganov, in their book *Tragediya sotsializma* ('The Tragedy of Socialism') provided a list of reforms that were critical for the development of capitalism, and which would have been impossible without the involvement of the labour movement:

    Rather than moralizing, we would like to point out that without the threat of revolution there would not have been factory laws in the nineteenth century, that without the October Revolution of 1917 there would not have been the 1919 international conference in Washington that resolved to make the shift to the eight-hour working day, that without the attempts to build socialism in the USSR the reforms of F.D. Roosevelt would not have taken place, and that without mass strikes and political agitation none of the humane and democratic features of which modern capitalist society in its most developed countries is so proud would have come to exist. The historical initiative for all these changes did not come from the ruling classes, and their implementation occurred despite resistance from these classes. (A. Buzgalin and A. Kolganov. *Tragediya sotsializma*. Moscow, 1992, pp. 107–8).

26. *Observer*, 24 November 1996.
27. D. Sassoon, *One Hundred Years of Socialism*, p. 739.
28. Ibid., p. 735. On the genesis of New Labour within the old Labour Party (as well as on the connection between the decline of the New Left and the growth of new realism) see L. Panitch and C. Leys. *The End of Parliamentary Socialism: From New Left to New Labour*. London, 1997.
29. W. Hutton, *The State We're In*, p. 277.
30. Ibid., p. 301.

31. *Disput*, 1997, no. 1, p. 2.
32. Ibid., p. 28.
33. W. Hutton, *The State We're In*, p. 326.
34. See ibid., p. 16.
35. *Inprecor*, February 1997, no. 410, p. 34.
36. *Socialist Campaign Group News*, January 1997, p. 10. The opinion polls and electoral results in Britain in 1997 also show (unlike previous elections) that in general Labour voters were more left-wing than the politicians. See K. Livingstone. 'Lessons of the General Election'. *Socialist Campaign Group News*, June 1997, p. 6. See also J. Rees. 'The class struggle under New Labour'. *International Socialism*, Summer 1997, no. 76.
37. *Svobodnaya mysl'*, 1996, no. 8, pp. 90–1.
38. *War Report*, January–February 1997, no. 48, p. 6.
39. *Red Pepper*, March 1997, p. 5.
40. *The Reconstruction and Development Programme: A Policy Framework*. African National Congress. Johannesburg, 1994, pp. 4–6, 14, 58, 119.
41. Ibid., p. 79.
42. *Building a Nation*. A Forbes Special Report on South Africa's Reconstruction and Development Programme. Pretoria, S.D., 1995, p. 60.
43. *The African Communist*, 1994, no. 138, p. 1.
44. Ibid., pp. 34–35.
45. Quoted in *Green Left Weekly*, 24 July 1996.
46. Quoted in *Green Left Weekly*, 3 July 1996, p. 20.
47. *Links*, July–November 1996, no. 7, pp. 85, 86.
48. Ibid., p. 100.
49. *South African Labour Bulletin*, March 1995, vol. 19, no. 1, pp. 73, 79.
50. *Green Left Weekly*, 3 July 1996.
51. W. Thompson. *The Left in History*. London and Chicago, 1997, pp. 123, 124. On strategic evolution of South African liberation movement see D. McKinley. *The ANC and the Liberation Struggle*. London and Chicago, 1997.
52. *Green Left Weekly*, 19 February 1997, p. 21. The way ANC dealt with popular protests was quite consistent with its own political thinking. 'Simply put, the ANC, guided by its leading members, has been unwilling to trust the very people it claims to represent; it has, in effect, been unable to trust real democracy' (D. McKinley, *The ANC*, p. 134).
53. *Links*, January–April 1996, no. 6, pp. 107–9.
54. Ibid., p. 112.
55. *Socialism and Democracy*, Summer 1996, vol. 10, no. 1, p. 8.
56. S. Clarke. *Keynesianism, Monetarism and the Crisis of the State*. Aldershot, UK, 1988, p. 364.
57. Quoted in *La Nouvelle Alternative*, June 1995, no. 38, p. 11.

58. Ibid., pp. 6, 7.
59. *Socialist Campaign Group News*, December 1996, p. 8. After the elections the official Socialist leadership also stated that there are extreme right-wing forces in Hungary 'which provoke justified fear' (*Transitions*, June 1998, vol. 5, no. 6, p. 13). What is missing, however, is the understanding that these forces become stronger exactly because of the policies of the 'realistic left' in office.
60. *Transitions*, July 1998, vol. 5, no. 7, p. 52.
61. *The Nation*, 23 December 1996, p. 22.
62. See *The European*, 9 December 1996. It is too early to draw up a balance sheet of Labour rule in Britain, but there is every reason to think that there too the new realism will lead to the growth of the radical right. Although Britain lacks a historical fascist tradition, as early as May 1997 a left-labour journal warned: 'One of the ironies of British politics is that a Blair government may stimulate a fascist revival' (*Workers' Liberty*, May 1997, pp. 28–9).
63. See Jacques Walker. 'Fascismes des annees trente et quatre-vingt-dix: allers et retours.' *Utopie critique*, 1997, no. 9, p. 29; J. Breitenstein. 'Offensive sociale du Front national'. *Le Monde Diplomatique*, March 1997, no. 516.
64. *New Left Review*, May–June 1996, no. 217, p. 126.
65. *Labour Focus on Eastern Europe*, Spring 1997, no. 56, p. 88.
66. K. Modzelewski. *Wohin von Kommunismus aus?* Berlin, 1996, p. 188. Original Polish title: *Dokad od Komunizmu?* Warszawa, 1993. The text quoted, however, is part of the final chapter that was written especially for the German edition.
67. *Labour Focus on Eastern Europe*, Spring 1996, no. 53, p. 65.
68. Ibid., p. 75.
69. *Independent*, 2 October 1996.
70. *Socialist Register 1996*. Ed. by Leo Panitch. New York and Halifax, 1996, p. 26.
71. *Iniciativa Socialista*, June 1996, no. 40, p. 19.
72. A. Buzgalin. *Budushchee kommunizma*, Moscow, 1996, p. 44.
73. D. Sassoon, *One Hundred Years of Socialism*, p. 656.
74. *Latinskaya Amerika*, 1996, no. 2, p. 48.
75. *Iniciativa Socialista*, October 1995, no. 36, p. 12.
76. *Segodnya*, 19 December 1995 (Short story 'The Lover of Power', translated by P. Grushko).
77. *Utopias*, 1996, vol. 4, no. 170, p. 128.
78. When in *The Dialectic of Change* (London, 1989) I wrote that leftists have to learn to retreat, my observation aroused furious indignation among radical authors. This position is reminiscent of the famous episode during the Second World War when in the Soviet Army all plans for retreat were kept secret. As a result, the army was incapable of retreating in organized fashion. Any

tactical reverse turned into a catastrophe, and withdrawal turned swiftly into panic-stricken flight.

2 De-Revising Marx

1. J. Derrida. *Specters of Marx*. New York and London, 1994, p. 39. It is important to note that Derrida's book in a certain sense signalled the change of the mood in the academic community and in the media. When the 150th anniversary of *The Communist Manifesto* came round, the mainstream press was full of articles praising Marx as a theorist of capitalism.
2. V.L. Inozemtsev. *K teorii postekonomicheskoy obshchestvennoy formatsii*. Moscow, 1995, pp. 13-14, 192. A readiness to view the achievements of the Western welfare state of the 1960s as irreversible is also present in more radical writers, for example one of the most notable of the independent leftists in the Russian parliament, Oleg Smolin. See O. Smolin. *Kuda neset nas rok sobitiy*. Moscow, 1995. For a polemic with Smolin see B. Kagarlitsky. 'Printsip Kassandry'. *Al'ternativy*, 1996–7, no. 4.
3. *Polis*, 1996, no. 4, p. 113.
4. W. Wolf. *Casino Capital: der Crash beginnt auf dem Golfplatz*. Koeln, 1997, S. 173.
5. W. Thompson. *The Left in History*. London and Chicago. pp. 1, 9.
6. Summarizing the results of the self-criticism of the German left in the early 1990s, André Brie writes of their uncritical adherence to 'the bourgeois understanding of progress' (A. Brie. *Befreiung der Visionen*. Hamburg, 1992, p. 25).
7. W. Thompson, *The Left in History*, p. 9. See also A. Giddens. *Beyond Left and Right: The Future of Radical Politics*. Cambridge, 1994, pp. 1–4, 69, etc.
8. See *PDS Pressedienst*, 13 December 1996, no. 50–1, p. 3.
9. F. Block. *Postindustrial Possibilities*. Berkeley, Los Angeles and Oxford, 1989, pp. 82–3.
10. Ibid., p. 82.
11. R. Burbach, O. Nunez and B. Kagarlitsky. *Globalization and its Discontents: The Rise of Postmodern Socialism*. London and Chicago, 1997, p. 142.
12. Ibid, p. 145.
13. Ibid., p. 150. As one of the authors of the book, I tried in my chapter on Eastern Europe to present a different vision of the alternative. However, these obvious contradictions in the text (to some degree noted in the foreword by Roger Burbach) lent the book a still more postmodernist air. An Australian reviewer of the book, Paul Clarke, noted with some derision: 'It seems strange to help to write a book you utterly disagree with, but

there you are' (*Green Left Weekly*, 19 May 1997, p. 25). The trouble was that the sharpness and irreconcilability of the contradictions between Marxism and the postmodernist interpretations of socialism became obvious to me while I was working with Burbach and Nunez.

14. K. Marx and F. Engels. *Sochineniya*, vol. 16 p. 31 (Marx on Proudhon in the newspaper *Sozial-Demokrat*, 1865).
15. *Svobodnaya mysl'*, 1995, no. 3, p. 75.
16. See J. Ditfurth. *Lebe wild und gefahrlich*. Koeln, 1991, pp. 52–3.
17. A. Giddens. *Beyond Left and Right*, p. 48.
18. O. Negt in P. Ingrao, R. Rossandra *et al. Verabredungen zum Jahrhundertende. Eine Debatte uber die Entwicklung des Kapitalismus und die Aufgaben der Linken*. Hamburg, 1996, p. 259.
19. A. Brie, *Befreiung der Visionen*, p. 124.
20. *Inprecor*, March 1996, no. 400, p. 9.
21. See A. Giddens, *Beyond Left and Right*; B. Kagarlitsky. *The Restoration in Russia*. London, 1995.

3 The Return of the Proletariat

1. J. Rifkind. *The End of Work: The Decline of the Global Labor Force and the Dawn of the Post-Market Era*. New York, 1995, p. 292.
2. See A. Gorz in: *After the Fall*. Ed. by Robin Blackburn. London and New York, 1992.
3. O. Negt in P. Ingrao, R. Rossanda *et al. Verabredungen zum Jahrhundertende. Eine Debatte uber die Entwicklung des Kapitalismus und die Aufgaben der Linken*. Hamburg, 1996, p. 259.
4. *PDS Pressedienst*, 1995, no. 28.
5. *Left Business Observer*, April 1996, no. 72, p. 7.
6. *L'Événement du jeudi*, 1996, no. 627, p. 59.
7. Even sociologists who are close to Rifkind in many ways dissociate themselves from this thesis. Hence Stanley Aronowitz stresses that when he speaks of 'the jobless future', he has in mind 'the disappearance of good jobs, not paid work'. The problem does not lie in the replacing of people by machines, but in 'the replacement of high-paying jobs with part-time, conyingebt [sic] and temporary work' (*Left Business Observer*, February 1997, no. 76, p. 8).
8. *Le Monde diplomatique*, June 1996, p. 6.
9. A. Giddens. *Social Theory and Modern Sociology*. Cambridge, 1987, p. 286. Giddens, who could never be described as a supporter of classical Marxism, is sure that the concept of 'high technology low employment' society is 'chimerical'. It is 'the result of an over-generalization from certain trends of the moment' (ibid., p. 296).
10. *New York Times*, 2 March 1996, pp. 1, 26.

11. *New York Review of Books*, 29 February 1996, vol. 43, no. 4, p. 47.
12. *New York Times*, 2 March 1996, p. 26.
13. Quoted in *Left Business Observer*, December 1996, no. 75, p. 7.
14. Ibid., p. 3.
15. Researchers associated with the German Party of Democratic Socialism note that the demand for jobs can grow dramatically as a result of the development of the 'social sphere', but that it is more advantageous for the German government to 'subsidize' mass unemployment than to carry out structural reforms that would lead to the creation of jobs. (S. Sikora. 'Leben ohne Arbeit.' *Utopie-kreativ*, 1997, no. 77). Here the class essence of social policy appears in full measure: unemployment is not only the consequence of technological change, but also the result of a conscious policy aimed (in complete accordance with Marx) at creating a 'reserve army of labour'.
16. *New York Times*, 2 March 1996, p. 26.
17. Ibid., p. 29.
18. F. Block. *Postindustrial Possibilities*. Berkeley, Los Angeles and Oxford, 1989, p. 102.
19. *Monthly Review*, July–August 1996, vol. 48, no. 3, p. 103.
20. *New York Review of Books*, 29 February 1996, v. XLIII, no. 4, p. 50.
21. *Korea Focus*, January–February 1996, vol. 4, no. 1, p. 84.
22. F. Block. *Postindustrial Possibilities*, p. 83.
23. *Svobodnaya mysl'*, 1996, no. 12, p. 91.
24. Ibid., pp. 92, 93. It is significant that the contradiction between creativity and the needs of capital is tearing even successful firms apart. Thus in 1996 crises arose as a result of which some of the best programmers of computer games were forced to quit companies which they themselves had founded (see *Hard'n'Soft*, 1996, no. 6 and others).
25. *Svobodnaya mysl'*, 1996, no. 7, p. 128; *Al'ternativy*, winter 1996–97, no. 4, pp. 99–100.
26. *Hard'n'Soft*, 1996, no. 2, p. 93.
27. F. Block, *Postindustrial Possibilities*, p. 87. Some economists even consider that the efforts by American corporations to retain traditional methods of control over workers under changing tchnological conditions lie 'at the root of the continuing inability of the United States to solve the productivity problem' (S. Bowles, D. Gordon and T. Weisskopf. *After the Waste Land*. Armonk and London, 1990, p. 156).
28. See V.L. Inozemtsev, *K teorii postekonomicheskoy obshchestvennoy formatsii*. Moscow, 1995, p. 222.
29. *Workers in Third World Industrialization*. Ed. by Inga Brandell. London, 1991, p. 2.
30. *Korea Times*, 30 April 1996, p. 1.
31. *Korea Times*, 25 April 1996, p. 2.

32. L.C. Thurow. *The Future of Capitalism*. New York, 1996, p. 183.
33. See *New York Times*, 2 March 1996, p. 28; *New York Review of Books*, 29 Feb. 1996, vol. 43, no. 4, p. 48.
34. *Monthly Review*, October 1995, vol. 47, no. 5, p. 16.
35. D. Bell. *The Cultural Contradictions of Capitalism*. New York, 1978, p. 198; see also: D. Bell. 'The Third Technological Revolution and its Possible Socio-Economic Consequences'. *Dissent*, Spring 1989, vol. 36, no. 2, p. 167.
36. *New York Review of Books*, 29 February 1996, vol. 43, no. 4, p. 50.
37. *New York Times*, 5 March 1996, p. A16–A17.
38. Will Hutton, *The State We're In*. London, 1996, p. xiv.
39. In the view of the German sociologist Joachim Bischoff, what is occurring on the threshold of the twenty-first century is not the forming of a new, post-industrial order, but merely a crisis of Fordism. A struggle is taking place to determine what solution will be found to this crisis (J. Bischoff in P. Ingrao, R. Rossanda *et al. Verabredungen zum Jahrhundertende*, p. 210; J. Bischoff. *Restoration oder Modernisierung? Entwicklungstendenzen des globales Kapitalismus*. Hamburg, 1995).
40. *Kommunist*, 1995, no. 2, p. 69.
41. Ibid., p. 70.
42. *New York Review of Books*, 29 Feb. 1996, vol. 43, no. 4, p. 51.
43. *Red Pepper*, March 1997, no. 34, p. 26.
44. See Sheridan Johns. *Raising the Red Flag*. Cape Town, 1995.
45. I. Wallerstein. *Unthinking Social Science*. Cambridge, 1991, p. 165.
46. Ibid., p. 166.
47. *Toward a New Global Civilization: The Role of the People and National/Regional Movements*. International Conference in commemoration of 30th Anniversary of Quarterly Changjak-kwa-bipyong. Seoul, 1996, p. 141.
48. L.C. Thurow, *The Future of Capitalism*, p. 179.
49. Ibid., p. 178.
50. This also suggests the conclusion that what is needed is not to reject or revise Marxism, but to rethink it, broadening the theoretical context.
51. V.I. Lenin. *Polnoye sobraniye sochineniy*, vol. 20, p. 112.
52. A. Gramsci. *Izbrannye sochineniya*, vol. 3, p. 157.
53. Ibid., vol. 3, p. 155.

4 New Technologies, New Struggles

1. See *Ekspert*, 29 April 1996, no. 17, p. 19.
2. *Moskovskie Novosti*, 1995, no. 68, MN-Biznes, p. 16.
3. *Nezavisimaya Gazeta*, 22 May 1996. American computer security expert Tsutomu Shimomura, famous for capturing Kevin

Mitnick, America's most wanted computer outlaw, recognizes that it is very hard in the computer world to discover theft 'for what is stolen is not the original piece of software or data, but a copy that the thief makes'. For the same reason it is hard to tell the exact damage. (Tsutomu Shimomura with John Markoff. *Takedown*. New York, 1996, p. 36.) The real problem is different. The problem is that the 'theft' at least in the traditional sense of the word actually *did not* take place and the damage is not the money or property *lost*, but supposedly lost profits of capitalist companies.

4. *Ekspert*, 29 April 1996, no. 17, p. 19.
5. See *Hard'n'Soft*, 1996, no. 11.
6. *Magazin Igrushek* (*Games Magazine*), 1996, no. 5, p. 64.
7. A. Buzgalin. *Budushchee Kommunizma*. Moscow, 1996, pp. 19, 20.
8. *Hard'n'Soft*, 1996, no. 4, p. 105.
9. *PC Week* (Russian edition), 26 September 1996, p. 55.
10. See *Kapital*, 15–21 May 1996, p. 9.
11. *Ekspert*, 29 April 1996, no. 17, p. 20.
12. *Hard'n'Soft*, 1996, no. 7, p. 92.
13. *Ekspert*, 29 April 1996, no. 17, p. 18.
14. *PC Week* (Russian edition), 26 September 1996, p. 55.
15. *Kapital*, 15–21 May 1996, p. 9.
16. *Ekspert*, 29 April 1996, no. 17, p. 20.
17. See John Frow in *New Left Review* (September–October 1996, no. 219). It is significant that although it would be more logical to subordinate the distribution of software to the norms of author's rights, norms which no one disputes, the capitalist rulers of the computer world have placed their stake on the more-than-doubtful principle of 'intellectual property'. The reason is simple – the quest for monopoly profits.
18. *Itogi*, 21 May 1996, no. 2, p. 57. While lagging in terms of technical modernization, Russia is outstripping other countries in creating a new generation of repressive organs. Russia has become one of the first countries to establish a special secret police for dealing with electronic networks – the Federal Agency for Regulatory Communications and Information (FAPSI). In 1998 the other Russian security agency FSB (former KGB) proposed its own project of obligatory monitoring of all electronic messages in the country.
19. *Itogi*, 1996, no. 19, pp. 25, 23.
20. *Zavtra*, 1996, no. 52. In this newspaper there are other, still more exotic declarations to be found. For example, about the fact that according to reports received from 'confidential sources', the brains of a number of members of the Russian government are directly linked to a supercomputer at the

University of Chicago that also directs the implementing of reforms in Russia.

21. *Kapital*, 30 October–5 November 1996, p. 22.
22. *Monthly Review*, July–August 1996, vol. 48, no. 3, p. 68.
23. *Links*, July–October 1996, no. 7, pp. 41–2. Shimomura complains that his work as computer security expert is getting harder because Internet and other networks 'were originally designed for sharing information, not protecting it'. That is why there are so many 'tempting targets for bandits and information highwaymen' (Tsutomu Shimomura with John Markoff, *Takedown*, p. 36). Isn't this really absurd: you first turn public space into private and then complain about people not respecting your exclusive 'rights'.
24. *Le Monde Diplomatique*, February 1997, no. 515, p. 27.
25. *Den' za Dnem* (Tallinn), 2 August 1996, no. 30, p. 4; http//sunsite.unc.edu/netchange/hotstuff/barlow.html
26. *Hard'n'Soft*, 1996, no. 7, p. 96.
27. *New Left Review*, September–October 1996, no. 219, p. 102.
28. *Hard'n'Soft*, 1996, no. 2, p. 89.
29. Ibid., pp. 89–90.
30. *Svobodnaya mysl'*, 1996, no. 7, p. 126.
31. E. Matzner and W. Street (eds). *Beyond Keynesianism: The Socio-Economics of Production and Full Employment*. Aldershot, 1991, p. 44.

5 The New Periphery

1. *Eszmelet-Consciousness*. Ed. by T. Krausz. Budapest, 1997, p. 202.
2. *Labour Focus on Eastern Europe*, Spring 1998, no. 59, p. 19.
3. *Eszmelet-Consciousness*, p. 107.
4. *Al'ternativy*, 1998, no. 3, p. 76.
5. S. Glazyev. *Ekonomika i politika: epizody bor'by*. Moscow, 1994, p. 87.
6. See *Al'ternativy*, 1998, no. 3, pp. 76–7.
7. *Transitions*, January 1999, vol. 1, no. 1, p. 29.
8. See Yu. Buzdugan. 'Sotsial-demokratichniy vibir.' Manuscript, p. 22.
9. S. Glazyev, *Ekonomika i politika*, p. 91.
10. *Vek*, 1999, no. 1.
11. Quoted in R. Medvedev. *Kapitalizm v Rossii?* Moscow, 1998, p. 125.
12. *Labour Focus on Eastern Europe*, Summer 1997, no. 57, p. 51.
13. V. Gushchin. *Prorokov net ...* . Moscow, 1994, p. 113.
14. *Transitions*, January 1999, p. 34.
15. *New Left Review*, March–April 1997, no. 222, p. 60.
16. Quoted in R. Medvedev, *Kapitalizm v. Rossii?*, p. 249.

17. *Transitions*, January 1999, p. 34.
18. *Nezavisimaya Gazeta*, 13 January 1999.

Conclusion

1. *New York Times*, 1 November 1998, p. 39.
2. *Financial Times*, 31 August 1998.
3. *Socialist Campaign Group News*, September 1998, p. 6.

Index

Index compiled by Sue Carlton